THE FUNDA
— OF —
BRAND
SERPs
FOR BUSINESS

*Google is Your New Business Card
and it is Up to You to Optimise Yours.*

JASON BARNARD

John Mueller, Webmaster Trends Analyst at Google, Via Twitter

John ✅ @JohnMu · 1h   ⋯
Replying to @jasonmbarnard
That looks awesome, well done! This always feels like one of those under-appreciated topics, people fret about titles on their pages, but who knew there was so much more you could highlight when users search for your name? Make it easy for folks to find the awesome things you do!

💬   🔁   ♡ 4   ⬆

Jason Barnard explains in his book The Fundamentals of Brand SERPs for Business *that business owners and brand managers often miss the opportunity to control their whole branded search engines results page. These days the strategy should not simply be getting indexed in search engines... the strategy should be to maximise visibility and to have your marketing message, your text, your images, your people, your products surfacing everywhere in page one of search results. Chapter after chapter, Jason explains the benefits and the strategy to follow to get there. Indeed, a great Brand SERP is great for your bottom line.*

Fabric Canel, Principal Program Manager - BING

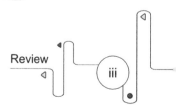

Jason Barnard's The Fundamentals of Brand SERPs for Business *will set you on the path to leveraging what is at everyone's fingertips in the online world... information about your brand.*

Ted Rubin,
Communications Transformation Strategist

There is no one more knowledgeable and authoritative in the subject of Google Knowledge Panels than Jason. His book demonstrates how important your brand is in Google search and how to ensure your brand in Google is represented in a manner your desire.

Jason is the Google Brand Guy, if he can only help me rank above Professor Barry Schwartz—I'd be even more grateful than I already am for his wisdom and generosity with the search industry.

Barry Schwartz, SEO Janitor
(SEO editor at Search Engine Land and Search Engine Roundtable and President of RustyBrick, Inc.)

Jason lays out an easy-to-understand explanation of what Brand SERPs are, why they matter to your business (and believe me, they do!), and how to easily improve yours. I have worked directly with Jason and his level of practical knowledge on this topic is unbelievable. In just a few weeks, his insights helped me vastly improve what my audience

sees when they Google my name. And now, this book is enabling me to do the same for my business: make my company look professional and convincing to my audience.

Scott Duffy, Top 10 Speaker: Entrepreneur.com

A big part of branding is based on the information people can find online about you and your business. That's why it is crucial to feed Google with accurate information. Jason's book, The Fundamentals of Brand SERPs for Business, *is a simple and powerful guide for those of us who are not SEO-savvy to create a more realistic, less technical, and marketing-focused approach to SEO.*

Ryan Foland, Speaker, Author, and Brand Consultant

How you appear in online search results is who you are… period. No one understands how to influence branded search results better than Jason Barnard. In his eye-opening new book, The Fundamentals of Brand SERPs for Business, *Jason reveals what drives online reputation results and shows readers how to stay ahead of the algorithms to positively influence how you show up to search engine users.*

**David Avrin Strategic Brand Development
Consultant and Author**

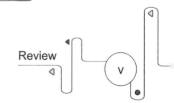

Jason has been very important in shaping our thinking at Yoast about Brand SERPs. This book is a great primer for those starting with optimizing their entities and brand result pages. This is probably one of the most important aspects of SEO these days, so why are you reading this and not the book itself yet?

Joost de Valk, Founder &
Chief Product Officer at Yoast

ISBN: 978-1-956464-10-8

TABLE OF CONTENTS

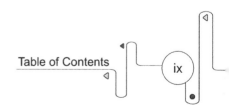

DEDICATION

Without any hesitation, this book is dedicated to Léonor-Jo Barnard. You are my favourite person in the whole world.

A secondary dedication (if I may) goes to Boowa and Kwala. You got me started on the internet in 1998, and despite being a figment of our imagination, in our 10 years together, you taught me more than is reasonable. In 2012, your presence on my Personal Brand SERP kick-started the entire Brand SERP "thing." The Brand SERP Guy thanks you. :)

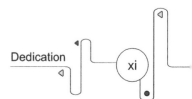

It's second nature these days to pull out your phone and search for a coffee shop when you need your next caffeine fix. Or, to type an address into Google to find directions. We don't even print out maps anymore because Google is at our fingertips, waiting to provide us with the best route and live traffic updates. As users, we take Google for granted, expecting it to always be there with answers. Google is a response delivery service and it *wants* to provide its user, you, with the best answers. So, how does this impact business owners?

Because Google is your new business card.

Google provides the results people see when looking up your business. Whether it's an existing client or a prospect who wants

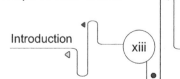

to learn more before taking the leap, Google is the go-to step in a person's journey to finding your company. As such, Google's representation of your brand is one of the most important brand messages they will see. Like it or not, the Google search result for your brand name is your "digital business card," so it needs to be positive, accurate, and convincing for your audience. And to achieve this, you need to be proactive and take control. It might seem daunting, but the process is accessible for the average person, particularly when you employ a few simple "tricks" to get the job done.

While most business owners understand the importance of their online image, many still balk at the sheer scale of the web, complexity of the task, and seemingly indecipherable technical concepts involved. This book may cover many concepts and terms you don't know (yet), and to help make understanding the content easier, I've included a glossary, footnotes, and other reference materials to guide you. Managing your "Google business card" doesn't have to be intimidating or complicated, and the benefits really do pay off big time.

An improved Brand SERP, the technical term for your digital business card, naturally leads to a significant increase in the control you wield over your wider online image. The whole process is easily manageable once you know the basic tactics, understand the crucial steps, and recognise the many acronyms associated with them. SERP is one such acronym.

SERP, or the Search Engine Results Page, is the web page you see after you enter a query into a search engine. When a user searches for a brand name, the search engine (Google, Bing, Yahoo, DuckDuckGo, etc.) shows them a Brand SERP, or the brand's Search Engine Results Page. Online brand images

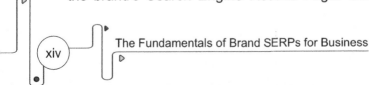

function similarly for individuals and businesses. For the purpose of this book, we'll be looking at Google's Brand SERP of your business.

The Brand SERP is a simple concept. But, like many topics with a clear premise, the devil is in the details and they add up to massive insights into your business, your digital strategy, and your audience. By addressing these small details, you'll build an improved business brand with a solid online strategy to better serve your audience. The key is to give due attention to each of these details, while also viewing them as effective pieces that improve the sum of the parts.

What is Google's "Raison d'Être"?[1]

Google's function is to provide solutions to user problems—it tries to provide the best information available online to fulfill a user's needs.

There are three types of searches we all perform:

1. Informational
2. Navigational
3. Commercial (transactional)

For each of these, Google builds its SERP to try to best serve the intent of the user. Informational and navigational searches are the central two searches for your clients and prospects.[2] When someone is seeking more information about your business, they will search your brand name with an **informational** intent to learn about who you are, what you offer, and if you are trustworthy.

---

1 Raison d'être: (lit.) reason for being/existing. In context, what's Google's primary purpose?
2 If you are interested in the broader picture of different search intentions, read this additional resource from my friends at Yoast: https://yoast.com/search-intent/

For a navigational search, the user already knows and is comfortable with your brand name, and they are looking to find your site. A **navigational** search occurs most often with well-known brands, such as Facebook. Even if you don't have a Facebook account, you know what it is and you know what the site offers. By searching for Facebook, you are only looking to navigate to the site.

Brand searches on lesser-known companies, such as my business Kalicube, are more often informational in nature because the brand and services aren't widely known. Google understands these different types of intents and knows which is most appropriate for your audience, so it builds your Brand SERP accordingly.

Google designs your Brand SERP to help users navigate to your site, find information about your brand, and access resources provided by your brand.

The entire internet strategy for your business stems directly from this one elementary statement. By understanding your Brand SERP and actively working to make it useful and valuable to your audience, you'll be building an incredibly solid, relevant, and effective digital strategy. However, very few business owners know how to get started, which puts them at a massive disadvantage. Google is the most comprehensible and helpful tool you have at your disposal to improve your business' brand. And ironically, it's free.

Google is by far the dominant search engine on the internet. It holds 86% of the global market share and handles approximately 3.8 million searches a minute, which amounts to roughly 5.6

billion searches per day (Desjardins; Johnson). This leaves other search engines, such as Bing and Yahoo, with a significant 14% of the global market share. To give you an idea of the vast scale of search engines, Bing serves search results to over a billion people every month (Clement). Since Google completes 5 times as many searches in just a day, the focus here will be on Brand SERP optimisation for Google. But remember, everything you do to improve your Brand SERP on Google will also help improve your Brand SERPs on Bing, Yahoo, and other search engines.

Internet searches are Google's game, so Google sets the rules. Though, contrary to popular belief, if you take a proactive Brand SERP approach, you can *lead* the game by educating Google. It aims to understand who you are and what you offer, and it wants to learn about your business from *you*. Google may not be human, but it is an incredibly sophisticated network of algorithms and is capable of learning.

Google is essentially a child trying to understand your brand message so it can accurately and fairly represent your brand to your audience. It's your job to educate Google using online content associated with your brand. Every time you add or change content on the web, Google reads and digests the information, and it learns more about who you are and what your brand is. This is where you lay out the ground rules and control your Brand SERP. If you provide a consistent message across all digital platforms, over time, Google will gain a better understanding of your brand and provide more accurate, relevant, and helpful information about you to its users.

With so much at stake, you cannot ignore Google's SERP for your brand. Many users looking for information about your business won't look beyond the SERP itself. Users are looking for

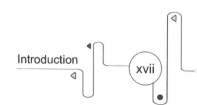

convenience, and Google packages up a summary of what it knows about your brand and provides this information on your Brand SERP. Since Google is essentially a reflection of the world's opinion of your brand, you need to ensure your brand is represented correctly.

When you search "Jason Barnard," you're met with this:

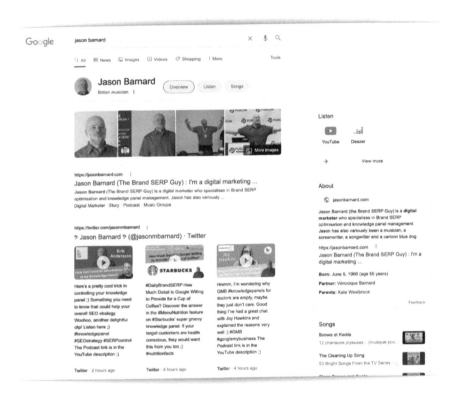

Google recognises me as the leading expert on Brand SERPs or "The Brand SERP Guy," *and* it presents the photos I want it to show. But these results are not just good luck. I studied the search engine and established how to educate Google so it correctly understands me and my personal brand, and represents the brand message I define. I didn't start with a big dream of demystifying Google.

Curiosity drove my research and led me to a deep understanding of how Google builds the Brand SERP and how it evaluates brand credibility.

A little background history: I graduated with a degree in economics and a minor in statistical analysis from Liverpool John Moores University. Then, I launched my first site in 1998, which is the same year Google was incorporated. Google and I kind of grew up together—not that Google has noticed!

I've been optimising content to perform well on Google since almost the very beginning of search engines on the internet. My first website was UpToTen, which offered educational games and activities featuring the cartoon characters, Boowa and Kwala. By 2007, the site was welcoming 5 million visits a month—a stunning 60 million total for the year 2007. 20% of these were organic visitors from Google searches. I realised I was able to dominate the SERP for generic queries like "kids games," "K-12 activities," and many more.

But I noticed there was a piece missing and business owners, myself included, were only doing half of the job. I had established a following for UpToTen, but when users searched the names to learn more, the results were not what I expected nor what I wanted. Google was getting my Brand SERP wrong.

So, I decided to figure out how to change the results being shown and help Google get things right. I Googled my name and was met with results on approximately 250 Jason Barnards from around the world: myself, a footballer, a dentist, a podcaster, a hockey player, a university professor, some other digital marketers, and still more. I realized I could use my skill set of dominating the Google search results for generic terms to intentionally control the results for my own (brand) name.

I had completed the hard part of using SEO to build a following for my site, but like most companies out there, I hadn't stopped to consider what users see when they search for the brand. If you've successfully captured the user's attention, your follow-through has to convince the user to continue. This involves the intentional optimisation of your Brand SERP.

I started with a "silly trick." One of the results was about my work in the 1990s as a musician. I played with the punk folk rock group, The Barking Dogs, and we did cover versions of several songs. One such cover was "Ace of Spades" by Motörhead. I provided this information to Google using some SEO techniques (see Chapter Six for SEO tactics) and Google "picked up" the information about me playing bass for our cover … and presented me as a musician in the original band! I'd added content of me playing the song and Google deduced that I was the bassist for Motörhead.

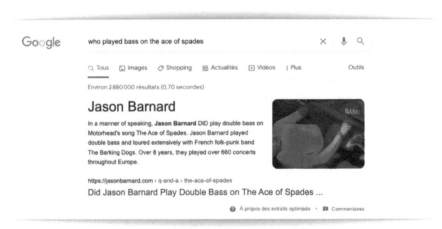

This was a comical test, but it does reveal an important point about Google—once Google accepts you as a trusted authority on you and your brand, you can "feed" it information with relevant content.

Here are some examples of how I have educated Google about myself:

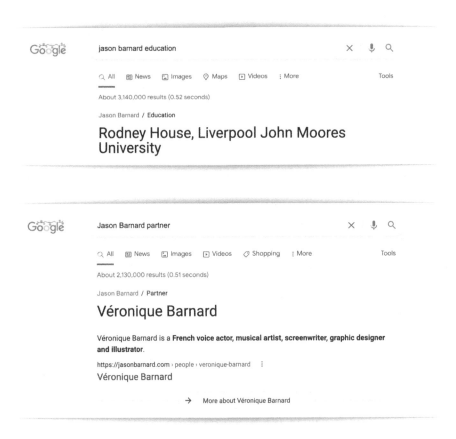

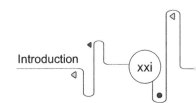

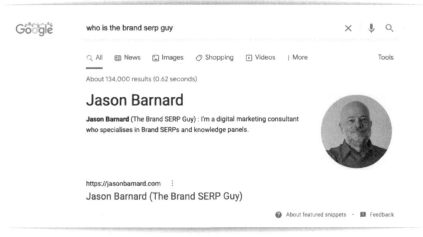

After my initial experiments, I realised brand owners can and should be educating Google about their businesses and brands. Brand SERPs in particular needed to be explored more for maximum business optimisation. My goals going forward were to:

- Make all references to me positive, accurate, and convincing
- Dominate the page results to "own" my SERP
- Prompt Google to show Rich Elements on my SERP[3]

As I began to master this process, I gained clients who saw my work and wanted to make changes to their own results. They saw the value of owning the brand narrative on their Brand SERP as I have successfully done. Working as a freelancer, I helped many brands over the next eight years. In 2015, as my client base grew, I professionalised my operations by founding Kalicube, honed my "trade" of Brand SERP optimisation, and in 2021, launched a

---

3 SERPs feature Rich Elements, such as a Knowledge Panel, Twitter Boxes, Image Boxes, Video Boxes, etc.

Software as a Service (SaaS) platform, Kalicube Pro. Kalicube Pro is the semi-automated, data-driven, pragmatic approach to Brand SERPs.

Kalicube Pro started as a set of tools I created to help me help my clients. It has now grown to become the go-to platform in the world for agencies looking to improve Brand SERPs for their clients, and an industry insights dataset containing 70,000 brands, over 10 million Brand SERPs, and a total of 200 million data points ("Kalicube Pro").[4] Kalicube Pro analyses a snapshot of your Brand SERP and uses a set of proprietary algorithms to establish where the underlying issues are, what needs to be improved, and which strategies will be effective.

Kalicube Pro is imagination applied to data; it combines pragmatism with creativity to gain insights into your Brand SERP, and provides strategies to leverage maximum benefit for your business.

Alongside the platform, I realized some clients needed a more in-depth understanding of the strategies and the reasoning behind them, so I recorded a series of video courses in 2019. In these videos, I walk the audience through the steps of managing their Brand SERP.

In all, I provide three levels of instruction:

1. This book covers the **fundamental theory** behind Brand SERPs.

2. The Brand SERP courses explore the **pragmatic approach** for invested business owners.

---

4   Figures collected from https://kalicube.pro, December 2021.

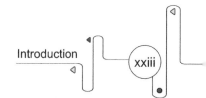

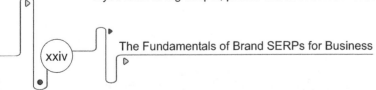

3. Kalicube Pro provides a **data-driven bespoke tasklist** to enable brand owners to take their Brand SERPs to the next level.

As you can see, the resources I offer have grown as my understanding of Brand SERPs has deepened and expanded.[5] All of these resources have one common theme: if you don't proactively feed it information about yourself, Google will make up its own mind based on the fragmented, often inaccurate information that it pieces together from around the web. This hodgepodge conclusion could show your audience an unrepresentative reflection of your brand based on what Google *thinks* is true. When it comes to business, you don't want to leave your brand's message to chance, so you need to proactively manage your Brand SERP with clear intent and determination. You need to educate Google.

By controlling your Brand SERP, you own the narrative of your brand and keep your potential clients focused on an accurate and convincing depiction of you.

Brand SERPs are the inescapable reality of our digital world. They provide the first, virtual face-to-face impression for your potential clients, and first impressions can be hard to overturn. By controlling your Brand SERP, you own the narrative of your brand and keep your potential clients focused on an accurate and

---

5   The Fundamentals Brand SERP course at
     https://courses.kalicube.pro offers much more detailed information,
     explanations, practical advice, and strategies for Brand SERP optimisation.
     If you want to dig deeper, please check out these lessons.

convincing depiction of you. For prospective clients, a good Brand SERP means a shorter path to conversion, higher conversion rates, and better client retention. For existing clients, it means better client engagement, easier upsells, and fewer clients leaving you for the competition.

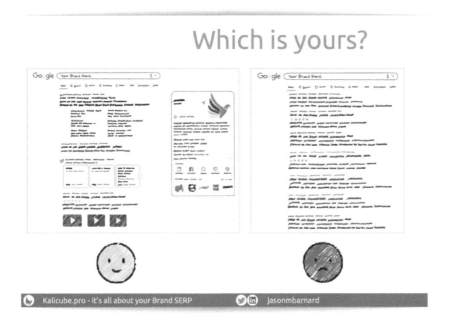

My mantra on Brand SERPs is straightforward and no-fluff, much like the process itself:

A good Brand SERP is good for your bottom line.
A great Brand SERP is great for your bottom line.

Your brand is your biggest asset in business, so you need your Brand SERP to represent it accurately. But more than that, your brand is an entity. When it creates your Brand SERP, Google

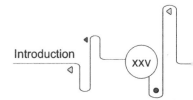

looks at your brand entity, *not* at your website. Your website is informative, but it's just one representation of your brand. Google is trying to understand the brand itself and determine the overall brand message portrayed online.

Business owners often see Google as an intimidating, complex force that's in control of their online business success. But this is *your* Brand SERP, *your* brand message, and *you* are the one in control.

There are many tactics at your disposal to take control of your Brand SERP, the most effective being:

- Optimising
    ◊ Your Homepage
    ◊ Rich Sitelinks
    ◊ Google Ads
- Improving
    ◊ Other Search Results (ones you control and those you don't)
    ◊ Your Social Media Accounts
- Employing
    ◊ Simple SEO Tactics
- Avoiding
    ◊ Cutting Corners with Cheats

Your starting line is the current impression your Brand SERP projects to your audience when they Google your business. Take a look at your Brand SERP now and ask yourself:

- What do I see?
    - ◊ An inaccurate message? A lack of compelling language?
- What did I *expect* to see?
    - ◊ More relevant results?
    - ◊ Your Twitter page, third-party corroboration, positive reviews, etc.
- What do I *want* to see?
    - ◊ Your brand dominating the search? Results that convince users to choose your brand?
    - ◊ Impressive third-party articles, 5-star reviews, social media platforms, etc.

Once you see the gaps and flaws, you can start to correct Google's understanding of your brand and "design" your Google business card, ensuring it positively reflects you and convinces your audience to do business. Your Google business card displays the world's opinion of you to your audience searching for your brand, so you need it to be as polished and convincing as your CV when applying for a job. The "job" here is landing the customer, and your Google business card is the CV they see.

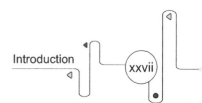

Since your Brand SERP is a reflection of the world's opinion of your brand, it's essentially an executive summary of your digital ecosystem. Your digital ecosystem consists of your site, your social media presence, the content you create and distribute, public feedback from your audience (including social media and customer reviews), and any third-party statements about your brand. Understanding the digital ecosystem of your brand starts with the Brand SERP, and you can easily build a solid ecosystem outwards from there. As you work through your digital ecosystem, you'll see your strengths, correct your weaknesses, plug the holes, improve your reputation, refine your brand message, and own your narrative.

In the ensuing chapters, this book covers the "why, what, and how" of every major aspect of Brand SERP optimisation. So please, read on.

CHAPTER ONE

Optimising Your Homepage

As an established businessperson, you've probably invested hundreds or even thousands of dollars to make an attractive and professional website for your visitors. The next obvious step in Search Engine Optimisation is making the site attractive to search engines so potential clients can find you on Google and Bing when they are looking for products and services like yours. Search Engine Optimisation (SEO) is an incredibly important strategy for your long-term online success. But before jumping with both feet into a massively ambitious SEO project, you need to do some foundational work first, such as optimising your homepage to secure the reputation benefits offered by a great Brand SERP when people Google your brand name.

Your homepage should appear at the top of your Brand SERP. It's the most appropriate response for a search of your brand, and Google can easily make that association. By making your homepage attractive to your audience on the SERP, you are ensuring their perception of your brand is already positive even before they navigate to your site or research your company more deeply. This is crucial since the people Googling your brand name are the most important people to your business: prospects and clients.

There is an exception to the rule "your website should rank #1 for a search on your brand name." Unfortunately, if you've established a business under an ambiguous brand name, or if you share your brand name with other companies, you'll have some competition for those top results.

Take "Yellow Door" for example. A door can be yellow *and* it's the name of several businesses: Yellow Door (Books and Resources for Early Years Learning), Yellow Door (Jewelry shop), etc.

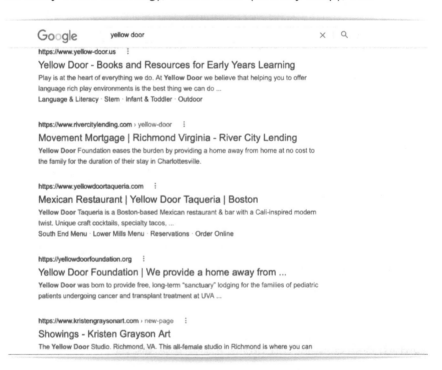

The Fundamentals of Brand SERPs for Business

That said, even with an ambiguous brand name, you can still use the following tactics to improve your Brand SERP.

The Meta Title and Description

A big part of your control is over the meta title and description. Meta title refers to the title you provide Google in the HTML (the blue hyperlinked title in the result). You can think of the meta title as the most basic education you give Google.

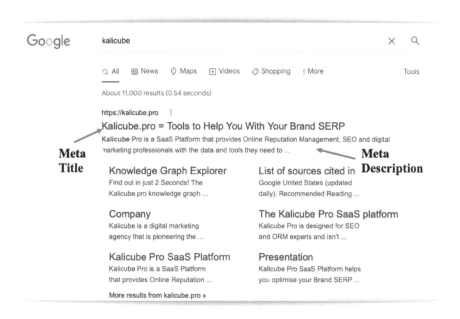

As you can see above, there's limited space for your meta title. Google only gives you about 60-70 characters, so each letter must be perfect and deliberate. My business's meta title is very precise and includes the name (Kalicube) and what I am offering (tools to help with Brand SERPs) in a way that draws the user's attention. Use the meta title to describe your brand and overall service being offered, as I've done. Try to include your unique selling point, but if it feels like a stretch, save it. The last thing you want to do is overwhelm your reader (client or prospect) and discourage them from visiting your homepage. The person is explicitly looking for you, so always start with your brand name and build the meta title from there.

As a whole, your meta title should be positive, informative, clear, and convincing. Use words that will emotionally resonate with an audience who already knows at least a little about you. You want to impress prospective customers *and* reassure existing clients in your limited space. Naturally, refining your meta title will take a few rounds of development and edits to create the most effective result. As your business grows and changes, be sure to update your meta title and description as needed so it continues to provide the best representation of your brand.

As an example, Amazon updated their own meta title for the first time in 17 years in June 2021. As you would expect, it was a move that their marketing department extensively researched, and the change was for a good reason: to create a more effective message to clients and prospects Googling their brand name, right at the top of their Brand SERP. For 23 years, the title emphasised sales and promotion as "Amazon.com: Low Prices in Electronics, Books, Sports..." The update changed it to "Amazon.com: Smile More, Pay Less." The new title places Amazon's brand front and center. The fundamental message conveyed on their Brand SERP is how the brand resonates with people searching for their brand name. I would like to imagine this change was influenced by my work on Brand SERPs. Is it a coincidence that Amazon made this change in 2021, a year I declared "the Year of the Brand SERP"? Perhaps. But allow me to dream.

Whatever Amazon's official motivations are, this new title is a massive shift and clearly conveys a human message that charms prospects, reassures clients, *and* provides the core benefits of their brand upfront. The change also shows that Amazon is no longer trying to sell right from the SERP. The focus is 100% on their brand message and brand image, making this an eloquent example of the correct approach to Brand SERP development.

Business optimisation is the end goal for these digital strategies. Since Google shows the meta description right below your meta title, it should expand on the message and follow the same approach: be clear, convincing, and on-brand. Bear in mind, the reader is a prospect or customer who already knows at least a little about you, so you have to project a resonating, clear brand message.

In order to do this, you need to utilize every space available. It's absolutely necessary for you to provide a meta description, otherwise Google will choose a section from your page. And that can be a disaster! Take a look at the example below and see the difference in quality for a description written by the company versus what Google will generate.

Description provided by the brand

https://www.yellow-door.net

Yellow Door - Publisher of innovative early years resources

We publish award-winning and multisensory early years resources, including hands-on resources, books and educational apps for EYFS and SEND.

https://www.theyellowdoor.com

The Yellow Door - Brooklyn's Home for Fine ... - Brooklyn

Follow us on Instagram @yellowdoor1. 1posts; 16969followers; 0following · 1posts · 16969followers · 0following.

Description chosen by Google

Don't let Google run wild. Help it by providing a description that promotes the most important and relevant aspects of your brand, including who you are, what you do, and who your audience is.

Ideally, your description should be between 160 and 200 characters. If the description you provide is too short (less than 100 characters), Google will automatically select a description from your page, and it may not be on-brand. If your description is too long, Google will truncate it and some of your message will be lost.

The meta description is the place to make your first selling point. Clearly outline what's unique about your brand and convince the reader to continue to your homepage. The language needs to build curiosity, indicate the importance of your brand, invite your reader in, *and* clarify the topic. It's not easy, but if you spend time on this task, you can convey an enormous amount of information in one short sentence.

In some descriptions, you'll see the brand has included references to customer reviews. Reviews can reassure potential clients and establish your credibility. Only include reviews if they accurately articulate your brand and unique selling point; otherwise, these reviews will lack the sufficient substance needed to convince your potential homepage visitors.

I know it's a lot to pack into 40 words (a 60-character title and 200-character description). Take your time to get it right—it's easy to write a compelling paragraph about your business but much harder to craft a powerful, comprehensive sentence. As Mark Twain said: "If I'd had more time I'd have written less."[1]

---

1   This quote is based on a translated letter written in 1657 by Blaise Pascal, French mathematician and physicist: "I have only made this letter longer because I have not the time to make it shorter." It has been repeated in various forms by Mark Twain, John Locke, Martin Luther, Henry David Thoreau, and many more.

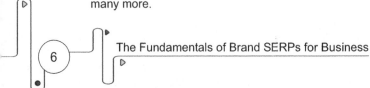

The meta title and description are important suggestions to Google about the content it should show its users on the SERP. When they are well written, representative of your brand, and helpful to your audience, Google will generally use your suggestions. However, bear in mind that Google has the final say, so it may choose to show different content in the SERP. All the more reason to spend time getting your metas right so you maximise the chances of Google using your message rather than creating its own.

Optimisation for Multi-Homepage Companies

If you are in charge of an international brand with multiple homepages or the same homepage but in different languages, you need to ensure your brand is consistent across the board.

Include equivalent resources and aim to incorporate the same "buzzwords" you use to describe your brand, adapted to the relevant language and culture. It's important to reflect the same brand image despite the language and cultural differences. Direct translations can convey an inaccurate message, so a native speaker should review your business homepage for every location.

For your brand to succeed, you need to establish a uniform message internationally—both for your consumer's sake and for Google's ability to understand your brand.

The Homepage Promise

Once your meta title and description attract the reader, your homepage needs to deliver on the promise. The majority of people landing on your page are going to fit into one of two categories: existing clients and prospective clients. Your existing clients will have a specific need they want to find answers to, so you need your website to be clear and easy to navigate.

Your prospective clients are assessing your offers and your credibility. They want their questions answered and they want to be convinced you're the right solution. Your content needs to clearly express the solutions you are offering, explain your services, and assuage any doubts they may have. The overall goal of your homepage is to adequately address the needs of the people who want to do business with you—current clients *and* prospective ones.

When you're designing your homepage and prioritising content, bear in mind what falls "above the fold." Unless people are engaged and invested, few will scroll down on a page for more information. Therefore, you want to make sure the top part of the page is perfect: put the most relevant and convincing content above the fold. If the top is catchy and informative, it may be enough to convince a site visitor to explore your site more and learn about your service/product.

Your homepage is crucial. It is a page like no other. A special case. Treat it as such.

An up-to-date and fresh homepage is key to maintaining a positive impression with existing and potential clients. It is a massive signal to Google that you are working to improve user experience and actively building your brand.

Since prospective clients will see your homepage when they are on the cusp of making the decision to do business with you, and existing clients will see the page again and again, it is well worth spending time to make it absolutely perfect. An up-to-date and fresh homepage is key to maintaining a positive impression with existing and potential clients. It is a massive signal to Google that you are working to improve user experience and actively building your brand.

Remember, your homepage is never the final destination for your site visitors—it's a stepping stone to other pages on your site. As such, you need to ensure you have an easy-to-navigate site for users to find the sections and pages on your site they are looking for. If your website proves frustrating to navigate, you may fail to convert prospects and possibly lose some existing clients too. Your homepage is a crucial place to reassure your "brand-aware" audience and introduce yourself to newcomers.

Once your homepage has been enhanced for a high-quality user experience, you can transition to optimising sitelinks to further improve your Brand SERP.

CHAPTER TWO

Triggering and Optimising Sitelinks

Optimising your homepage is the single most important and easy-to-implement improvement for your Brand SERP. But if you want to provide a positive experience for your audience on your Brand SERP, the next step is to develop Rich Sitelinks under your homepage. "Sitelink" is the technical term for the hyperlinks to website subpages. On a Brand SERP, these sitelinks appear under the homepage and are designed to help users navigate to specific pages on the brand's site. Take a look at the Brand SERP for the grocery chain, Aldi:

Aldi's Rich Sitelinks include quick navigation to their featured deals, list of products, careers, and the option to coordinate grocery pickup and delivery. These links provide an improved user experience on the Brand SERP, and by making the shopping process easier, Aldi may have secured more sales simply through their sitelinks.

Sitelinks that Address the User's Needs

Google includes three essential types of links in the sitelinks of a Brand SERP:

- Navigational
  - ◊ Contact Us
  - ◊ Client Login
  - ◊ Store Locator, etc.
- Informational
  - ◊ About Us
  - ◊ Blog
  - ◊ Terms of Service, etc.
- Commercial
  - ◊ Pricing
  - ◊ Special Offers
  - ◊ Products
  - ◊ Services, etc.

These links address the different reasons most users search for a brand name. By placing these links on your Brand SERP, your

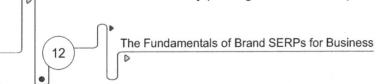

clients can obtain the information they are looking for without taking a detour through your homepage. This direct access from the Brand SERP is surprisingly powerful, especially since it improves the user experience.

For Kalicube, the sitelinks look like this:

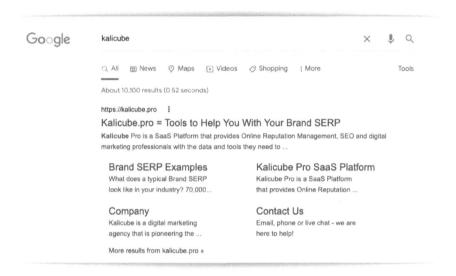

Here, Kalicube directs users to the Kalicube Pro SaaS Platform, a presentation of the company, information on Brand SERPs, and an easy way to contact us. For both prospects and existing clients, this is a great Brand SERP user experience.

Without sitelinks, a potential client is likely to skim right over your business's homepage and move onto your competition. Users are looking for information and convenience. They don't want one without the other, and Google is aware of this. Within your own Brand SERP, you should work to ensure that Google includes Rich Sitelinks, since this will encourage more traffic to your website.

A Rich Sitelink refers to an expanded version of your sitelinks. This includes the blue link text *and* a description (called a snippet). My example sitelinks are considered Rich Sitelinks because they provide some context for the users without the need to click and navigate. Because of their nature, Rich Sitelinks have some basic pros and absolutely no cons:

Pros

- Easy for you to get.
- Easy for you to influence.
- Helpful for your audience.
- Gives you control over more SERP real estate.
- Provides you with more text to project your brand's message.

Cons

- You only have influence over sitelinks, not control. *But,* if you follow the tactics outlined in this book, there are no disadvantages to sitelinks.

As you can see, there's a lot to gain with no risk involved in developing Rich Sitelinks, and having them will vastly improve your overall Brand SERP.

Astonishingly, only about 50% of brands have Rich Sitelinks on their Brand SERP. Therefore, Rich Sitelinks are an easy way for your brand to stand out from the competition. This low-effort task will give you a competitive advantage and these sitelinks provide a highly visible place for you to expand on your brand message.

Your homepage meta title and description only allocate about 40 words, whereas with Rich Sitelinks, the number increases by well over 200% to about 100 words. You can use the extra space to present to your clients and prospects cherry-picked positive and helpful representations of your brand and services. In addition, people using your Brand SERP to navigate can click your sitelinks to go directly to the page they're looking for without stopping first at the homepage. Nothing says opportunity like convenience.

Google is all about convenience, and it understands the value of its users having direct access to different site pages via sitelinks. Therefore, Google will provide sitelinks whenever it can. Sitelinks act as both a representation of Google's understanding of your website and also key contributors to the success of your Brand SERP.

Facebook is an excellent example of a brand with successful sitelinks. When users search for Facebook, Google clearly understands the user and the site, and it includes Rich Sitelinks that offer clear navigation for Facebook users *and* business owners looking to connect with those users as consumers:

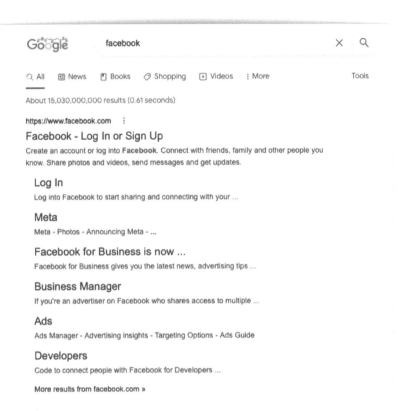

Right away, Facebook sets itself above the competition by providing user-friendly navigation on its Brand SERP. Your business won't have Facebook's extensive reach, but Rich Sitelinks work the same way for every business—they make life easier for your audience and help make your business the obvious choice.

There are several reasons to curate Rich Sitelinks:

1. They're above the fold, so they're seen by everyone who searches for your brand on Google.

2. They provide an extended brand message.
   ◊ *You* influence the links.
   ◊ *You* control the content.

3. They help your audience.
   ◊ Sitelinks improve navigation, which creates a positive user experience.

4. They look professional.
   ◊ Lacking Rich Sitelinks looks unprofessional and unconvincing.

5. They dominate the top of your Brand SERP.
   ◊ With Rich Sitelinks, you control the top 30% to 40% of your Brand SERP, whereas without them you control 10% at best.

6. They "kill off" blue links.
   ◊ Rich Sitelinks take up more space, which pushes the less relevant results in the Brand SERP to the next page.

Including Rich Sitelinks will give you an edge over competitors since they improve the user experience while also communicating your brand message to potential clients. The more Brand SERP results you influence or control, the better brand representation you get and the fewer distractions there are for your existing clients.

Rich Sitelinks are High Priority for Brand SERPs

When a user searches for something, Google's algorithms determine the most relevant and useful pages for the user. Google processes a user's geolocation, search history, type of device, etc. to provide the results best suited for each particular user. As you can see below, even a brand name as straightforward as "yellow door" will have very different results in the US compared to the UK.

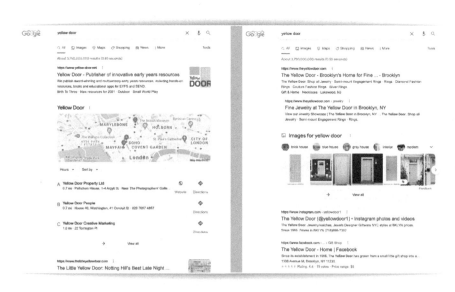

Google analyses its users, your brand, and the interactions between the two so it can provide the best results. By creating Rich Sitelinks, you'll be giving Google more fodder to inform and help your audience, which includes the essential information about your business: who you are, your office/outlet locations, employee profiles, recent articles, reviews, company calendar, how people can interact with you, pre- and post-sales, FAQ, etc. Behind these sitelinks are informational pages that are often forgotten by business owners, but are absolutely vital for both consumers and Google.

The Fundamentals of Brand SERPs for Business

It's a win-win-win situation—the consumer has the ease of navigation, you increase your control of your brand message, and Google gets the opportunity to represent you correctly.

One incredibly important aspect of your website is how you organise and group pages. This is important for every aspect of your SEO strategy, including Rich Sitelinks on your Brand SERP. Google's ability to produce relevant and helpful sitelinks depends on its understanding of the role each page plays and the solution it provides to the user. The content of the page is evidently crucial, but where the page appears within the structure of the site is also essential and often overlooked.

The technique you need to employ for organising your pages is called siloing. Much like silos on farms, website content silos refer to stacking or organising the material vertically by type and topic. In the context of websites, siloing makes sense for humans and also makes processing information on your site easier for Google and will vastly improve your chances of getting Rich Sitelinks on your Brand SERP.

Despite the intimidating term, creating silos is simple, and the final product looks like this:

- https://words.com/topic1
    - ◊ https://words.com/topic1/sub-topic1
    - ◊ https://words.com/topic1/sub-topic2
- https://words.com/topic2
    - ◊ https://words.com/topic2/sub-topic1

With silos, Google can collect the information in your site more easily and their algorithms can digest the information more effectively. This means Google will better understand who you are, what you offer, and who your offers are pertinent to. When completed correctly, siloing will enable Google to provide the best possible Rich Sitelinks, which will improve your Brand SERP. But intelligent, logical, and systematic siloing will also improve your overall SEO strategy.

Once you have siloed them correctly, how do you optimise the pages themselves for Rich Sitelinks? There are three major optimisations you need to apply to each page to make it a good Rich Sitelink candidate for your Brand SERP.

Firstly, write descriptive meta titles and descriptions. The rules here are similar to those for the homepage. Be accurate, clear, and concise. The title and description are shorter (less than 30 characters for the title), so you'll need to be even more concise than you were for the homepage. It's important to note that since the homepage title and description already contain the brand name and communicate the overarching brand message, these sitelink titles and descriptions merely need to describe the role of the page and why it might be helpful to the user.

Secondly, include a paragraph in the page itself that is visible to the user and describes the role of the page. This might seem pointless for a page such as "Contact Us." However, friendly and encouraging text is great for the user and is one of the most important aspects Google takes into account when choosing Rich Sitelinks.

Finally, some technical improvements help enormously. The details of these are outside the scope of this book, but your web developer can help you: ask them about web page subtypes in Schema Markup such as the "About" and "Contact" page.

Many of the pages that naturally appear as Rich Sitelinks on Brand SERPs, such as "Login," "Contact Us," or "About Us," are ignored in a typical SEO strategy. This is the correct practice because these pages generally only appear for brand searches, and SEO strategies usually prioritise non-branded search terms. This means you can focus on making those pages perfect for their exclusive role as sitelinks for your Brand SERP.

Your homepage and sitelinks are results you control, and they are the easiest and most visible way to improve your Brand SERP quickly.

The pages you use to drive traffic in your wider SEO strategy (such as product pages, category pages, blog articles, events, etc.) should continue to be optimised for that purpose. It really isn't possible to optimise for Rich Sitelinks on Brand SERPs and SEO for non-brand search terms at the same time. Therefore, it's illogical to optimise these pages for sitelinks and "kill" money-making SEO strategy traffic for the sake of a slightly better Rich Sitelink. Instead, rely on a great meta title, meta description, and quality content. As long as those are all relevant to your brand, the Rich Sitelink on your Brand SERP will look pretty good.

Your homepage and sitelinks are results you control, and they are the easiest and most visible way to improve your Brand SERP quickly. But improvements to your Brand SERP aren't always quite so straightforward.

After developing your sitelinks, you can begin building your social media profiles, which appear on your Brand SERP and are partially in your control.

CHAPTER THREE

Managing Social Media

Social media is ubiquitous. It is a massive, ever-evolving "beast" with users of all ages and backgrounds. As such, a social media presence is crucial for business success, regardless of the products and services you offer. The key to social media is choosing the right platforms. You need to choose sites with the right demographics—platforms where your audience naturally gathers and engages with each other. For example, LinkedIn for B2B, TikTok for GenZ, Pinterest for a B2C audience, etc.[1]

Consider "mom and pop" shops. Most often, they don't use social media, and their business comes from a steady stream of locals and some customers who are just passing through the area. These businesses have a limited reach, and as a result, they have a limited consumer pool. This approach works fine for "mom and pop" shops, but if you're looking for a wider consumer base or prominent business presence, then you need to integrate social media into your business strategy.

---

1   B2B, "business to business," is a company that provides services to other businesses.

B2C, "business to consumer," is a company that sells directly to individual consumers.

Every business (including "mom and pop" stores) can benefit from a presence on relevant social platforms. An active social presence is a great tactic to reach new audiences in a strategic way. Some business owners may dismiss social media as trivial and unnecessary, but social media platforms are an incredibly powerful marketing tool and have a major presence on Brand SERPs.

Social media's influence can't be ignored. Over 3.96 billion people, or about 51% of the world's population, use some form of social media to connect with others, entertain themselves, or gather information ("Surprising Social Media Statistics"). The majority of social media users participate daily on their favorite platforms.

On average, social media profiles occupy over 30% of the real estate on a Brand SERP, and 5 of the top 10 sites on Brand SERPs are social media platforms ("Kalicube Pro"). If you have social media accounts, even semi-dormant ones that you rarely update, you need to manage them intelligently since the profile pages of those accounts are very strong candidates for ranking on your Brand SERP.

Be aware that these social media profiles are trickier to manage than your own website. Since you are restricted by the rules and requirements of the platform, you only have semi-control over the actual content of your profile page. Furthermore, you only partially control what happens on social media, and you have no control over how your audience interacts with your content.

The Aspects within Your Control

In terms of what Google displays on your Brand SERP, your direct control is limited to the title of your business profile and the description of your brand. This varies slightly depending on the platform, but generally the system is the same. Make sure you review what the different platforms display on your Brand SERP, so you can optimise the information on your social media profiles accordingly. Note that the information Google displays beyond the title and description can include many elements such as the number of followers, reviews, the date of the most recent activity, and much more.

Social Media as a Medium

- Of the 7.7 billion people on the planet, there are more than 3.96 billion social media users.
  - ◊ 4.5 billion of the world population has internet access, with 80% of web users on social media ("Surprising Social Media Statistics").
- MySpace was the first social media platform to reach 1 million users, which it did in 2004.
  - ◊ MySpace is considered the first platform to establish social media as we know it today (Ortiz-Ospina).
- In the US, adults spend more than 6 hours a day on digital media (Ortiz-Ospina).
  - ◊ Internet usage has increased since the COVID-19 pandemic as people use social media platforms and apps to keep in touch during lockdowns and restrictions.

◊ 90% of US adults say the internet has been essential or important for them in the pandemic, and 81% say they have used video call applications/sites (with varied frequency) since February 2020 ("The Internet and the Pandemic").

• Social media removes the restrictions of location and time, allowing people to connect with others across the globe.

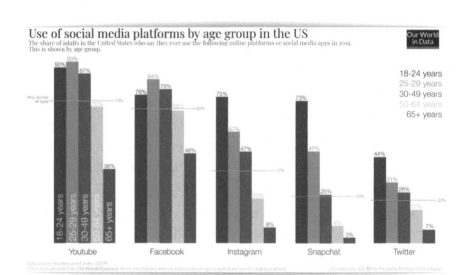

Use of social media platforms by age group in the US
The share of adults in the United States who say they ever use the following online platforms or social media apps in 2019. This is shown by age group.

The Fundamentals of Brand SERPs for Business

The Bonuses of Social Media

At a basic level, social media is an easy win for your Brand SERP. Profiles on multiple platforms are a great way to have control over relevant content beyond the scope of your homepage. There is no absolute rule, but brands can have 2, 3, or even 4 social profiles displayed on their Brand SERP. Combined with your homepage and Rich Sitelinks, this means an immense amount of control over what your audience sees when they Google your brand name. Every aspect of your account matters—from the posts you make to the people you follow to the colors in your profile. They all contribute to your overall brand message.

And there is a *massive* bonus. By working on your social presence and publishing relevant, compelling content, not only will these platforms become a permanent fixture on your Brand SERP, but the people you are engaging with on those platforms are much more likely to visit your website to learn more about your products and services. For myself, Kalicube, and our clients, we have found that an active social media presence improves the Brand SERP and also brings in new clients directly from those platforms.

These days, many businesses hire someone specifically for social media marketing/content management. Google may not know if you hire someone dedicated to creating content, but it will judge the value of your content and consider whether or not it's a valuable and helpful resource for users. If you want a particular social media account to rank on your Brand SERP, then, once you have optimised the profile itself (always the first step), direct your energy to making the account attractive to users and Google. This isn't a set-and-forget effort, but a process of creating relevant content that intrigues your audience and then actively interacting with them. Once your profile starts ranking on page 1 for a search of your brand name, your Brand SERP will look better and encourage your audience to visit your social platforms, thereby creating a circle of mutual benefits between social media, your brand, and Google.

Now the question becomes: "Which social platform is relevant for me?" For gaining visibility on business social media accounts, Facebook, Twitter, Instagram, YouTube, and LinkedIn are the more effective sites. Some of this depends on your audience, industry, and country; however, most often these social media platforms are easy opportunities because they're relevant for the people who Google your brand, and Google knows it. Even if your company's profile has limited activity (which I do not recommend), a profile on one of these platforms will often rank because of its relevance to your brand, your industry, and the natural strength of these platforms in Google's eyes.

The dominant social platforms on your Brand SERP will not necessarily bring you the biggest "client bonus." Industry-specific sites can provide a larger and more loyal following with the trade-off being that you reach a smaller audience. It's best to build your profiles across a number of social media platforms in order to increase your visibility and Brand SERP.

But what about the other platforms such as TikTok, Tumblr, or Pinterest? These can be incredibly powerful in some industries and regions, but they can also be a waste of time if your audience does not naturally congregate there. For whichever platforms you think are the most appropriate for your industry, it is vital to do some research about them first. Make sure you are leveraging the right platforms for your audience, industry, and geo-region before you invest time and resources into specific platforms. You can look at the Brand SERPs for your competitors and see which platforms dominate to get an idea of where to spend your time. At Kalicube, we automatically track this for our clients and offer insights into which platforms dominate in their industries and country, and what strategies will work in their specific cases.

Since every company has access to social media and the majority of people in the world actively use these platforms, your business will greatly benefit from using social media as a marketing tool. You'll be generating new business while improving your Google Business Card!

The Prominent Social Media Platforms

 FACEBOOK

- 69% of surveyed adults use Facebook on a regular basis.

- On your Brand SERP, Google includes page/account name and description.

- Facebook sometimes provides sitelinks for the Brand SERP.

  ◊ Engagement is key to having your profile be included on your Brand SERP.

- Any reviews posted to your Facebook profile have the potential to be displayed on your Brand SERP. This is great news *if* your customers are satisfied.

- 23% of surveyed adults use Twitter on a regular basis.

- 80% of Twitter users are affluent Millennials.

- On your Brand SERP, Google includes a recent tweet and/or the date of your last tweet.

- When creating a profile, choose your Twitter handle to be as close to your brand name as possible in order to maintain a consistent image across your digital ecosystem.

- Content from your Twitter profile feeds directly into Google.

  ◊ To see a fun demonstration of this, Google search "What is Jason Barnard's Twitter trick?"

- An active Twitter profile with great audience participation naturally offers Rich Elements, known as Twitter Boxes.

  ◊ You have control over the brand message in those Twitter boxes.

  ◊ This element looks great and will capture the attention of your prospects.

  ◊ A profile and consistent posting provides Google with content for your Brand SERP and beyond.

 **INSTAGRAM**

- 40% of surveyed adults use Instagram on a regular basis.

- There are 500 million daily active users and 1 billion total accounts.

- Instagram images receive 23% more engagement than Facebook images.

- Instagram is more difficult to rank on your Brand SERP.

  ◊ It requires *immense* user participation and regular posts.

- Instagram has a smaller audience reach and is less flexible as a marketing tool compared to other platforms.

- On your Brand SERP, Google automatically includes your username, the facts and figures of your profile.

  ◊ If you have a high number of followers and posts, this is great. Otherwise, it may diminish your brand image.

YOUTUBE

- 81% of surveyed adults use YouTube on a regular basis.

- 400 hours of video are uploaded to the platform every minute.

- 1.3 billion people regularly use the platform.

- On your Brand SERP, Google includes the video title, your channel title.
  - ◊ If you can, choose the same name as your other social media profiles.
- Results often include either a description or the latest video you've published.
- YouTube can trigger YouTube Boxes on your Brand SERP similar to Twitter Boxes.
  - ◊ These are very convincing to Google and your audience.

in LINKEDIN

- 28% of surveyed adults use LinkedIn on a regular basis.
  - ◊ This number is likely to increase dramatically since most job applications (in the US) specifically ask for a URL to your LinkedIn profile.
  - ◊ This platform is mostly for professionals and businesses.
- 45% of people earning more than $75,000 USD have a LinkedIn account.
- 64% of social referrals to corporate websites come from LinkedIn.
- On your Brand SERP, Google includes the brand name.
  - ◊ A tagline offers you the chance to include a brand message, which may appear on your Brand SERP.

Sources: Pew Research Center and Broadband Search

The Fundamentals of Brand SERPs for Business

Putting Your Profiles into Action

Social media removes the boundaries of physical borders and provides your business with the chance to build a wider audience base as you connect with interested parties. Social media platforms are dominated by mobile users, which is a big plus. People use social media on their smartphones more naturally and easily than they will use your site. Whether they're standing in line for coffee or ignoring people on the metro, many people are constantly reading on their phones. You have a massive opportunity to grab their attention when they are on the go, and this habit provides you with endless possibilities to create content while *you* are on the go. I cannot emphasise enough how important it is to take full advantage of your reach and appeal to the audience you have as well as potential consumers.

Be sure to focus on people who will be truly interested in your offers. Appealing to people who find you irrelevant is a huge waste of time and resources; it's better to have a small, highly relevant, highly engaged social audience than a vast audience that never interacts with you.

So, what should you do? Don't just talk about your business, services, and offers. Instead, make sure the majority of your content is helpful and enjoyable for your audience. Concentrate on starting conversations with your audience about topics they are interested in using videos, audio, and images (memes and GIFs in particular), *and* creating opportunities for audience participation.

If you're in the auto business, a social media post could ask people to comment with their favorite cars, either from movies or ones they themselves have owned. It's a little silly and won't directly lead to sales, but interactions that invite further engagement will increase brand awareness, improve the perception of your brand, create a larger audience reach, and tell Google that your account is a valuable resource for people searching your brand.

Likes, comments, and sharing posts build your credibility with Google and create more content for Google to include on your Brand SERP. That's not to say your posts should all be playful or off-base; they should relate to the products and services you offer, but do so in an interesting and inclusive way. Take a look at these prominent companies and how they encourage interaction with their Twitter and Facebook audiences:

Uber ✔ @Uber · Sep 9

Generosity isn't a competition. But we're still keeping score. Which riders are the bigger tippers?

New York	62.7%
Houston	24%
Atlanta	13.3%

549 votes · Final results

💬 47   🔁 8   ♡ 20

Show this thread

Domino's Pizza ✔ @dominos · May 28

Based on your birth month, which pizza topping are you?

Jan: pepperoni
Feb: olives
Mar: sausage
Apr: bacon
May: green peppers
Jun: extra cheese
Jul: jalapeño
Aug: pineapple
Sep: mushrooms
Oct: ham
Nov: spinach
Dec: steak

💬 340   🔁 120   ♡ 619

Domino's Pizza ✓
December 28, 2020 · 🌐

TRUE or FALSE: There are 34 million possible pizza combinations and you order the same thing every time.

🔵 Chat with Domino's Pizza in Messenger. [Message]

👍❤️ 9.2K   1.1K Comments 409 Shares

👍 Like   💬 Comment   ↪ Share

Delta ✓ @Delta · Sep 8
Which Delta logo is your favorite?

The Fundamentals of Brand SERPs for Business

Delta Air Lines ✪ I
September 13 at 10:00 AM · 🌐

Our newest destination? A carbon-neutral future.

292   93 Comments 31 Shares

👍 Like   💬 Comment   ↗ Share

The content you create needs to function on multiple levels. It needs to captivate and inform, and the medium itself needs to be varied, which means including rich media such as GIFs, images, and videos. Videos are a particularly effective format since they are multi-purpose; they can be repurposed as images, sound, text, or used in their original video form. Think about it: when you scroll through social media, do you stop to read the paragraph of text, or do you pause at the brightly colored image with giant text on it? Social media is meant to be visual; some platforms rely on it more than others. Instagram and YouTube are all about the visuals, so it's a no-brainer. Twitter and Facebook are more text-based, but users often include videos or photos. In almost every case, text-only posts get less attention and participation than the ones with images or video.

From a business perspective, by focusing on rich media on social media, you'll build a solid social presence while naturally providing a solid, powerful digital ecosystem, which will trigger Rich Elements on your SERP that are more enticing and convincing than plain text.

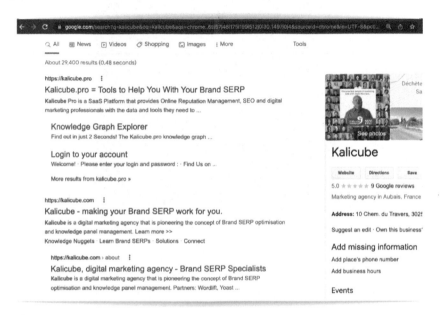

The Fundamentals of Brand SERPs for Business

Although social media profiles only offer your business semi-control over the results, the platforms' capacity for engagement means they are easy to retain on page 1 of your Brand SERP, and they are a positive representation of your brand over which you have a great deal of influence.

From a Brand SERP perspective, actively working on multiple relevant platform profiles helps Google get a better sense of your business and brand message. With more information to pull from, Google is able to represent your brand better, as well as understand where and when you can provide value to its users. Although social media profiles only offer your business semi-control over the results, the platforms' capacity for engagement means they are easy to retain on page 1 of your Brand SERP, and they are a positive representation of your brand over which you have a great deal of influence. Social media is not guaranteed to rank, but after your own site, they are the most reliable candidates for your Brand SERP and provide indispensable benefits. Beyond social media platforms, you should also explore other online spaces; though most only offer partial control, they can still contribute to your Brand SERP and help you reach a larger audience.

CHAPTER FOUR

Improving Results with Partial Control

Results you only partially control or you don't control at all (*see Chapter 5*) are a double-edged sword; they can either earn you extra credibility with your audience and Google or create confusion about your brand and its message.

Any content that is accurate, positive, and corroborates your brand message is a positive signal for your audience. This is true for your own content and your social profiles, as well as results you do not directly control. These results can add credence because they are independent from your brand and offer an outsider's perspective on your business. Google recognizes these impartial, third-party results and values them more because of it, making them great candidates for your Brand SERP. Since Google's bottom line is the user experience, it wants to select the most trustworthy brands for a user's SERP. Users trust Google as unbiased and independent, so its representation of your brand is vital for the credibility of your business.

The flip side is that if the content is inaccurate, it causes confusion and uncertainty. These less-than-favorable results will create a negative impression for Google and its users. Because Google and your audience perceive these results as independent, they can be challenging to remove. If the results are inaccurate and you can change them or have them changed, then the priority is to improve the results as much as possible. If the results are negative and you cannot have them corrected or reworded, then you will need to push those unwanted results off page 1 of your Brand SERP page and down and out of sight on page 2.

Users trust Google as unbiased and independent, so its representation of your brand is vital for the credibility of your business.

To create your Brand SERP, Google merely synthesizes and reflects the world's opinion of your brand. So naturally, a positive online presence will yield a positive reflection on your Brand SERP, and negative noise around your brand can easily sour your results. Public perception of your brand is vital to your business success, so it's essential you land and maintain positive mentions from third-party sites.

Some of the results you may have limited control over include:

- Informational Sites
  ◊ Wikidata, Crunchbase, Wikipedia
- Industry-Specific Sites
  ◊ Organisations and associations relating to your industry

- Commercial Sites
  ◊ Amazon, eBay, etc.
- Media Sites
  ◊ Such as websites where you're a guest blogger or contributor
- Review Platforms
  ◊ Yelp, Google, Trustpilot, Amazon, Glassdoor, Indeed

As you analyse your Brand SERP, identify which third-party results boost your brand's image and which ones are negative or confuse your brand message. You should make changes to improve these results to the extent the platform allows you to. If the result is positive but slightly imperfect, tweak it. If the result is negative or confusing, correct it if you can.

But be warned: you could fall into a potential trap of inadvertently "waking up" bad results. By updating these unwanted results, you "wake" them and make them more timely. This will encourage Google to retain them, or worse, push them higher up your Brand SERP. If you cannot make the result positive, accurate, and convincing to your audience, then you should leave it alone and work to improve the results below it. You can push them up the Brand SERP, thus pushing the bad result down. This technique is called "Leapfrogging."

Work your way through the sites where you have partial control and see where you can make improvements and where you need to push the result to lower pages. The Kalicube course, "Dealing with Negative and Sub-Optimal Results," explains the Leapfrogging technique and how to address the results you need to bump down to a lower page, but for now, let's focus on the results you can improve.

Addressing the Results You Can Improve

You need to ensure that informational sites provide accurate content about your brand since your audience and Google will use these sites to learn basic information about you and to better understand your brand. Some of the top sites are Zoominfo, DnB, Wikidata, Bloomberg, Crunchbase, and Wikipedia. They are default choices for doing preliminary research, and an inaccurate or negative representation of your brand on sites like these can ruin your Brand SERP and perhaps cost you a customer.

Informational sites will sometimes appear on page 1 of a Brand SERP but more often on pages 2 and 3. This means they are generally less visible than your own website and social profiles. As you review these sites, make sure the information is accurate, positive, and complete. You should include links to your own website and social media accounts, both to ensure that Google understands the resource is about your brand and also to encourage users to visit your pages. If you have the option, edit the meta title and description. The meta title should be kept brief with just your company name, a short synopsis of your brand, and the site name.

Unlike the other sites, Wikipedia is not an option for most companies. Basically, unless you are a recognised innovator in your industry, you don't "deserve" a page on Wikipedia. Creating your own page is a fool's errand. If the human editors on the site judge you as insufficiently "notable," your page will be removed within two weeks. If your company already has a Wikipedia page, you can make minimal edits, such as adding references and correcting inaccurate information. For the most part, you're not supposed to edit a Wikipedia article, especially one where you are a biased party.

Wikipedia is an encyclopedia and, as a rule of thumb, should only contain pages about entities that a significant number of users would spontaneously research. Further, it deals in facts only, and your page will be removed if the editors determine that it is not of real value to Wikipedia users, or if they believe it has been edited with a biased viewpoint. If you want your own Wikipedia page, take the time to build your digital ecosystem and online presence first. Being recognised as an authority in your industry by an independent third-party site or authoritative sources will make your brand "worthy" of a page, according to Wikipedia's standards.

Profiles on industry-specific sites are great candidates for ranking on a Brand SERP and are an ideal way to create results you partially control in addition to your social media profiles. In many ways, these sites are "better" for your Brand SERP than dominant platforms since Google perceives industry sites as highly relevant to your audience and are therefore quite valuable to include on your Brand SERP. Despite their smaller reach, these sites still carry influence in Google's eyes due to their topical relevance.

Examples of Industry-Specific Sites and Social Media Platforms

Lawyrs.net: A social media platform for lawyers to share legal updates and create international referral networks.

ResearchGate.net: A collaboration platform for scientists to share their projects and research and get feedback from other experts.

Sermo.com: A US-based online physicians community that addresses topics from patient care to practice management to medical advancements.

LinkedFA.com: A social networking site for financial and insurance professionals and investors.

ActiveRain: The largest international social media platform for real estate professionals.

Gust Launch: A platform specifically for start-ups that offers tools and connections to like-minded entrepreneurs.

Sources: https://www.threegirlsmedia.com/2021/04/21/5-useful-niche-social-networks-for-professional-industries/

https://www.socialmediatoday.com/content/industry-specific-social-networking-fad-or-future

Don't Overlook the Influence of Industry-Specific Sites

There are 3 reasons to integrate more industry-specific sites into your digital ecosystem:

- They rank well today.
    - ◊ Because they're relevant to you and important to your audience, Google prioritises these sites for inclusion in a Brand SERP even over generalist sites such as Crunchbase or Wikidata.
- They will rank better in the future.
    - ◊ Google is focusing more and more on topics, ontologies, and categorisation, so these sites will carry more and more weight as time goes by.
- They are a powerful corroboration for Google.
    - ◊ Google uses the information on these sites, and because they are topically relevant, they really help Google gain confidence in its understanding of who you are and what you do.

Although not always very "sexy" for your audience, these additional sites can provide you with a "control cushion" on your Brand SERP: multiple results on pages 1-3 where you have partial control to keep less positive (and possibly damaging) results out of sight on pages 4 downwards.

Limited Control with Commercial Sites and Reviews

Commercial sites where your brand has a profile page only offer limited control because your brand is operating under the umbrella of a larger company. Take Amazon and eBay for example: they tend to prioritise their brand over yours even though they are selling your products. For these sites, you typically can't control a great deal in the meta title or description, but you can choose which products are featured for your brand. I generally don't recommend trying to have this type of site on your Brand SERP, unless selling through them is a major part of your business strategy.

Other sites with profile pages for brands can offer you some control. An example of this type of site would be if you're posting articles on a third-party blogging platform or news outlet. Much like commercial sites, these sites typically offer limited control and will tend to prioritise their brand name over yours. The amount of control you have will vary from site to site, but if you have some control, use it to project a consistent brand message.

Review platforms tend to rank well and easily on Brand SERPs because Google knows most shoppers consider the reviews of a company before they make a purchase. Google will try to rank what we call "service reviews," or pages that collect reviews about the quality of a company's customer service, rather than pages with reviews about the company's products.

Review sites are a big source of angst for many companies due to the lack of direct control. But if your customer service is top-notch, there's no reason to be scared of them. You do not have direct control, but you can heavily influence how they look on your Brand SERP.

In general, if a customer is satisfied with a product or service, they are unlikely to leave a review. It's the outliers, those who are *exceptionally* satisfied or dissatisfied, who leave their feedback. You can counter this tendency and turn review sites into great credibility signals for Google and your prospects by encouraging all of your satisfied customers to leave a positive review on these platforms. Simply include a candid request in post-sale emails: "Happy with our service? Please leave us a review on Trustpilot," and include a link to the review page for your business. If you are a bricks and mortar business, you can suggest clients leave a review, or even give them a flyer with step-by-step instructions explaining how to leave a review. As a rule of thumb, you should be aiming for an average review score of 4.5 out of 5.

Popular company review sites include Yelp, TrustPilot, BBB, and Tripadvisor, but there are also many industry or country-specific sites that, because of their topical relevance, can often be better "targets." Look at the big players but also seriously consider these niche review platforms since they are highly relevant to your industry and your audience. You can start by prioritising any review platforms that currently rank on the first 2 to 3 pages of your Brand SERP, since these are the ones Google currently considers important and they are the most visible to your audience. You can also look at your competitors' Brand SERPs to see which review platforms rank for them. If Google sees them as relevant for your competitors, they are likely to be great candidates for your Brand SERP too.

Here are two examples of highly relevant review platforms:

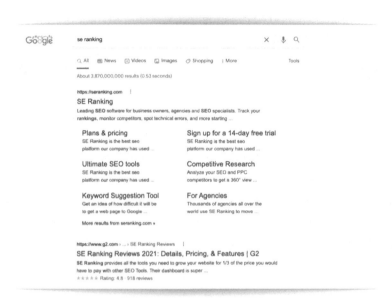

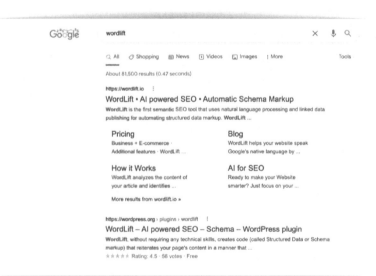

The Fundamentals of Brand SERPs for Business

Job sites with employee reviews, such as Indeed and Glassdoor, are another type of review platform that easily ranks on Brand SERPs. Unfortunately, reviews on these sites can be outrageous and wholly inaccurate, and because you are dealing with current and ex-employees, it is a delicate task to overtake bad reviews with good reviews. It's one matter to ask for a review from satisfied customers: explicitly asking an employee for a great review is tricky and can easily backfire. As a rule of thumb, 3.5 out of 5 is a good average score for employee reviews and it is difficult to score higher.

Generally speaking, I don't recommend trying to change these results even if they are unflattering or negative since it is unlikely you will succeed. A better approach is to use the Leapfrogging technique I mentioned earlier to push these job sites down the rankings and out of sight, preferably to page 3 or below. Reviews from former employees can negatively impact your Brand SERP and should therefore be monitored.

ALDI Reviews with Jobs   Review this company

Job Title   **Location**

| All | ∨ | United States 5,576 reviews | ∨ |

Ratings by category

2.8 ★ Work-Life Balance   3.8 ★ Pay & Benefits   3.2 ★ Job Security & Advancement   3.0 ★ Management   3.0 ★ Culture

Search reviews   **Sort by**   **Language**

| | Search | Helpfulness   Rating   Date ↓ | Any ∨ |

Found **5,576** reviews matching the search See all 8,700 reviews

---

Clear All   Full-time, Part-time ✕   English   ⇄ Filter

Found **6,992** of over **8,297** reviews   Sort   Popular ∨

3.5 ★★★✦ ☆ ∨

57% Recommend to a Friend   75% Approve of CEO   Jason Hart 1,958 Ratings

ⓘ Your trust is our top concern, so companies can't alter or remove reviews.   ✕

Pros
"Good pay treated well by above management" (in 1084 reviews)
"Great pay with substantial increases in year 3 and 5 of service" (in 638 reviews)

Cons
"They don't offer a work life balance" (in 606 reviews)
"Long hours required to be worked" (in 502 reviews)

ALDI Careers

Our Strategy What if a grocery store challenged the typical retail business model? We provide our customers with a focused range of... – More

Store Staff   ›

Warehouse   ›

District Manager   ›

Office and IT   ›

Reviews by Job Title

Store Assistant (624)

ALDI
3.4 ★★★✦ ☆
5576 reviews

ALDI Ratings

3.4 ★★★✦ ☆
Average rating of 5576 reviews on Indeed

2.8 ★ Work-Life Balance

3.8 ★ Pay & Benefits

3.1 ★ Job Security & Advancement

3.0 ★ Management

3.1 ★ Culture

Headquarters
Batavia, IL

Employees
10,000+

Revenue
More than $10B (USD)

Industry
Retail

Website
Facebook | ALDI company website

Cultivating an online presence is more complicated than creating a user-friendly homepage and attractive social media accounts. Your Brand SERP reflects Google's evaluation of your online presence, and the bigger your company grows, the more important a diverse digital ecosystem becomes for your Brand SERP.

A larger digital ecosystem means more results have the potential to appear on your Brand SERP, and while most are entirely or partially in your control (social media, review sites, and your own website), some results offer you no control at all. However, even when you have no control over results linked with your brand, you can still take measures to improve the results.

CHAPTER FIVE

Dealing with Results You Don't Control

Now let's take a look at results over which you have no control. Whether they are positive, neutral, or negative, they all require your attention. Content from relevant and authoritative third parties tends to rank well on your Brand SERP because Google values the independent assessment of the brand.

It's every business owner's dream to have a great article from a trusted and authoritative source ranking on the Brand SERP. Praise from a third-party source will feel like acknowledgement for a job well done, but the alternative scenario is a nightmare: seeing an inaccurate, negative representation from a third-party site in plain view of your audience when they search your brand name. Here, it may feel like a moment to despair and throw in the metaphorical towel, or worse, to angrily strike out and try to discredit the publisher. Instead, the best strategy is to calmly approach the source: the author of the negative mention. While content from third parties does tend to rank well on your Brand SERP and you can't control its presence, you can appeal to the person behind the review.

Your Brand SERP only contains about a dozen sources or less, and these are the most influential web pages about your brand (both for your audience and for Google).

With any third-party content, you want to work to get the meta title and description to be as good as possible so the result is positive, accurate, and compelling on your Brand SERP. Ideally, you also want the content in the page to be positive for your brand, not only because people may click on the result and read the content of the page, but also because Google pays particularly close attention to third-party mentions of your brand. Since you have no direct control, you need to appeal to the owner of the site to modify their content. If the result is positive but the title and description on your Brand SERP could be better, then your aim is to get the author to improve them. If the result reflects negatively on your brand, you can try to convince the person to tone the message down to a more neutral response.

Approach with Caution (and Class)

For results outside of your control, you can't storm the author's inbox with your demand to make changes. Think about it. Even if you knew the person behind the content, you wouldn't dream of asking a professional favor that way. Improving these third-party results (positive or negative) requires strategic action on your part. Before anything else, you need to establish a relationship with the third-party author.

Like any relationship, it's important not to rush the process, so make a genuine attempt at building a connection with the author. By far the best way to start is with an introduction by a mutual acquaintance. This approach gives you a great kickoff since a mutual acquaintance will give you credibility in the eyes of the author. Rather than having a metaphorical "foot in the door," the door will be held wide open for you. Of course, this isn't always an option, in which case you'll need to establish a relationship on your own merits without a recommendation to elevate you. The question is: "How?"

If you cannot get a personal introduction and recommendation, the next best way to approach the author is in person. While this may seem a little aggressive to some, in an online world that leans towards detachment, a face-to-face meeting is increasingly powerful. When you talk to someone in "real life," you have the chance to be much more than a two-dimensional online profile and make a good impression on them. This method is especially effective if you and the author attend the same type of events, such as industry brunches, conferences, and workshops. In this context, the introduction is more natural and has a greater chance of success since it allows you to strike up a conversation and establish a connection before you ask them for your favor.

If a personal connection isn't an option, either through a mutual acquaintance or face-to-face introduction, then reaching out on social media is your best bet. First, ensure your profiles are professional and articulate your business's brand—visiting your profile will be the person's first move before they decide whether to interact with you. The relationship is tenuous (at best), so you realistically have just one chance to "get your foot in the door."

When you do reach out, the author will likely look at your profile, so you need to ensure they see the best possible version of you.

LinkedIn is often the most suitable option for reaching out because it has a massive focus on professional relationships. When you connect on LinkedIn, it is a good idea to add a personalized note to your request, assuming you have an interesting subject for the recipient. If you can't think of a genuinely worthwhile message, send nothing with your connection request.

Whatever you do, avoid directly talking about your Brand SERP problem. A first message with a "pitch" candidly asking the author for a favor is not attractive and puts pressure on the person, which makes it easy for them to ignore you. At this point, the idea is just to get your name and face on their radar. The discussion about your problem comes later.

If the author is also active on Twitter or another major platform, follow them there too. It's important not to overdo your efforts and come across as overly persistent or downright creepy. Be reasonable in your expectations for this connection: you're a stranger, and the author doesn't owe you anything. Give the author time to respond and start a conversation. Once you've chatted back and forth a couple of times, then you can ask for your favor.

There's no definitive "right" time to approach the author with your favor. You have to "read the room" and get a sense of whether the author will be open to your request or will find it pushy or impertinent. Remember, this author's mention of your business is a part of your Brand SERP, and you can't improve the mention without their help.

If you rush the connection or offend the author, you've lost your best chance. You are going to ask this person for quite a big favor, and people generally don't do favors for strangers. You need to build a relationship before you ask.

There's an Art in Asking

Then, when you do finally ask your favor, you need to phrase it in a way that engages them. Most often, this means outlining the changes as mutually beneficial. They have to feel comfortable in the relationship and see the value the change will bring them. Some people will help out of the kindness of their hearts. This is the exception, not the rule. Most often, people don't want to expend energy without some kind of benefit in return.

Consider the two email approaches below:

1. *"Hello, my name is Jason Barnard, and I tell people how to make their Brand SERPs better. I'm pretty well-known and the work I do is pretty revolutionary."*

2. *"Hello. Your recent article about SEO tactics and using social media platforms has generated a great discussion about my work with Brand SERPs. Thank you for the positive mention. The article currently ranks incredibly well on searches for my brand name, which is really favorable for my business. Perhaps we could chat about how we can make your article work even better for both of us."*

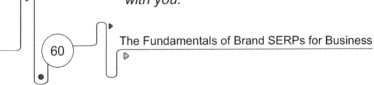

There's a distinct difference in these two approaches. The first example is very egocentric and uses what I call an "I, me, mine" approach. That's how most people naturally speak and write, but communicating with others from this point of view is a big turn-off and can be isolating and off-putting. Most people get tired of being talked at and react more positively to being talked to. If you're asking a favor, you need to put yourself in their shoes and pivot from egocentric to empathetic if you want to make your request appealing to the author.

The second email attempt places the emphasis on the other person right from the start. You mention their work and thank them for the positive mention. From there, you mention the effects of the article and propose making some uncomplicated, mutually beneficial changes. This approach shows the link between them (their article) and you (your brand). By including "we" in the final sentence, you create the idea of a mutual bond, perhaps even a team spirit, for moving forward.

Here's another set of examples:

1. *"I think your article gives a great overview of what Kalicube offers. We recently updated our product specs, so please update your article accordingly."*

2. *"Your article gives a great overview of what Kalicube offers, and you have sent quite a few happy customers our way over the last year. On behalf of the entire team, thank you. I should mention that we updated our product specs last week, so the information in your article is no longer 100% up-to-date. Could you spare a little time to chat so I can share the details? Please let me know if this is possible and, if so, when would suit you. Looking forward to chatting with you."*

The first is a fairly typical message, but it's unlikely to succeed. Yes, you mention their article, but you reference the article only in relation to your work. Once again, the emphasis should be on the author and their company, not you and your business. The request to update the information is direct, bordering on being too blunt while also managing to be dry and unoriginal. The final example makes more sense and is significantly more likely to be successful.

Here, you start with a positive mention about their work and continue with how it has helped your relationship. At this point, you have made them feel good about themselves and you have created an implied relationship. Now, you can naturally indicate that the article is no longer accurate and suggest chatting to update the information. In most cases, content like this doesn't qualify as a misrepresentation of the truth—the article information is merely outdated and inaccurate now, which is something most authors would want to remedy. In the email, you acknowledge that their article and positive mention brought you business while gracefully voicing your request. The request demonstrates flexibility and awareness of the time the author would sacrifice to update the article. The friendly tone is engaging and conveys an authentic desire to connect and build a relationship. This email doesn't guarantee a response, but the approach will vastly increase the likelihood of hearing back from the author.

An obvious faux pas in this situation would be to try and use a template email. We're all guilty of trying to save time by copying and pasting the exact language we've successfully used before into a new email and then changing some details to make it "personalised." Your Brand SERP contains only a dozen sources or less, and these are the most influential web pages about your brand (both for your audience and for Google). Don't try to cut corners here because this favor, if accorded, will bring a hefty positive boost to both the audience's and Google's perceptions of your brand.

As with any professional favor, you need to make your request relatable, relevant, and open. You can follow a loose structure, but the email shouldn't feel stiff or rehearsed—it should be unique and address the person, their point of view, and allow them some "wiggle room." Since each case is unique, if you want your message to be compelling, your approach needs to be personalised. You only have one shot at establishing a connection with the author, so take the time to do it right.

Once you have established a relationship, you need to convince the author to make changes to their representation of your business. To achieve this, you need to demonstrate the value the changes will bring them (directly or indirectly).

When reaching out, keep in mind that you're essentially asking the author to do free work to make you and your brand look better. This is a simplified version of the scenario, but you get the point. You may get lucky and the author will be generous and change the meta title and description because they're kind-spirited, but in most cases, in order to get results, you'll need to clearly define the benefits these changes will bring to the author.

Emphasise the Benefits for Them

An improved, more relevant meta title and description will make the page more attractive to users on Google's search results, thus increasing the probability of a user clicking on the result instead of a competitor's. Clearer and more accurate content will improve the page's Google rankings for relevant terms—both improving current rankings and also expanding the "keyword pool" for the page (i.e.

it will start ranking for additional search queries). Those are all big wins for the author.

There are many easy wins for ranking on Google for all sorts of search queries and keywords. Once you understand them, you can include them in your pitch. When explained well, the value of these changes is easy for the author to appreciate. Done intelligently, the benefit they derive from implementing your advice is reason in and of itself. The fact that you also benefit is secondary for them. *That is the trick.*

Examples of easy SEO wins for the author include improving meta titles, meta descriptions, headings, subheadings, and adding visuals. These are often minimal efforts for the author and will potentially bring them significant benefits. At the very least, making these adjustments will improve the content's value for their users. Essentially, you are offering the author the most incredible low-risk, high-reward changes.

If they are open to the idea of changing the meta title and description, offer to provide these changes for them. This involves time and effort on your part but offers massive paybacks. Not only will they be more open to implementing your suggestions since you reduce the work on their end, but you can ensure the changes project a message on your Brand SERP that is 100% positive, accurate, and convincing. Even so, don't be selfish in your changes; write the metas so they look great for your Brand SERP and also appeal to the author's audience. Get the balance right, and both parties get a big win on Google.

If you provide value to the author and you can clearly demonstrate the value to them, you'll get the changes you want, you'll both benefit, and then, who knows? Perhaps your relationship will continue to develop and you'll do business further down the line.

If the author is resistant to making changes, don't keep pushing. Reel in your request and ask for just the core change you need. You can point out that changing the meta title and description doesn't change the visible content on their page (the metas are only seen on Google's search results). The integrity of their content remains untouched.

If they are still reticent, then there isn't much of an appeal you can make. It's the author's content and their site, and they don't owe you anything. If the author rejects your request, handle it with grace. You never know if you'll need to contact them again, or if they may change their mind later. Don't burn any bridges you hope to stand on in the future. By making a tactful exit, you leave the door open to try again in a few months, perhaps with more specific details on how the changes will benefit them.

Making a direct appeal to the content's author is often the best and most effective approach to improving results you have no control over.

Even if the author doesn't modify their metas or their content, you haven't lost anything except negligible time. And, you can still take action to reduce the impact on your Brand SERP if the result is negative. You can move the result down and off your Brand SERP using the Leapfrogging techniques from the Kalicube course, "Dealing with Negative Content." Nonetheless, making a direct appeal to the content's author is often the best and most effective approach to improving results you have no control over.

Changes to third-party sites you don't control may seem small and inconsequential, but they carry influence over your overall Brand SERP. Every detail on your Brand SERP counts, and every time you improve your Brand SERP, you look more convincing to your audience and more credible to Google, which is all that matters in the long run.

When paired with other SEO tactics, seemingly insignificant steps combine to produce first-page results. What many people perceive as details—a consistent brand message, positive sentiment around the brand, social media participation, Rich Elements, communication with third parties, etc.—are, in fact, fundamental to your business online. Each small detail adds up and gradually pushes you above your competition in the eyes of users and Google.

CHAPTER SIX

Triggering Rich Elements (SERP Features)

When you search for your favorite comedian or look up a TV show, Google will likely show you a SERP with videos embedded in the results. The SERP is the "answer" to your query and Google uses videos to create a better user experience. As the internet matures, so do the search results. Google is becoming an increasingly multimedia results engine. These multimedia results are known as Rich Elements or SERP Features: videos, audio, images, etc.

Any multimedia content you produce to support your online business, including social media posts, videos, images, and podcasts, has the potential to trigger Rich Elements. In fact, Brand SERPs often feature rich multimedia elements from third-party sites. Therefore, you'll need to monitor results you control, semi-control, and do not control, as they will all influence the Rich Elements Google chooses to include on your Brand SERP.

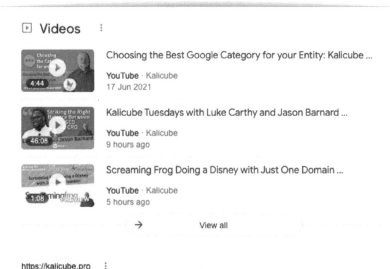

▶ Videos

Choosing the Best Google Category for your Entity: Kalicube ...
YouTube · Kalicube
17 Jun 2021
4:44

Kalicube Tuesdays with Luke Carthy and Jason Barnard ...
YouTube · Kalicube
9 hours ago
46:08

Screaming Frog Doing a Disney with Just One Domain ...
YouTube · Kalicube
5 hours ago
1:08

→   View all

https://kalicube.pro

Kalicube.pro = Tools to Help You With Your Brand SERP

Kalicube Pro is a SaaS Platform that provides Online Reputation Management, SEO and digital marketing professionals with the data and tools they need to ...

Rich Elements are a real boon for your Brand SERP because they are much more visually appealing and they take up more space than other results, such as basic blue links. Since they take up more space (SERP real estate), incorporating Rich Elements will reduce the total number of results per page, which means there are less results you'll need to manage on the traffic-heavy and all-important first page. Rich Elements are also an opportunity to show your "most attractive face" to your clients and prospects when they Google your brand name, since Rich Elements make your Brand SERP look more professional and convincing. They can establish authority and credibility, while offering relevant information in different mediums.

There are dozens of Rich Elements on Google search results, but only some will be candidates to appear on your Brand SERP. Twitter Boxes, Image Boxes, Video Boxes, Rich Sitelinks (*as explored in Chapter 2*), Top Stories, "People Also Ask" panels, and Related Searches are the primary contenders for Brand SERPs. As of May 2020, 15% of all Brand SERPs contained no Rich Elements, and by November 2021, the number had dropped to just 6% ("Kalicube Pro"). Rich Elements are becoming prevalent on Brand SERPs all around the world, and the total number has doubled in the past year:

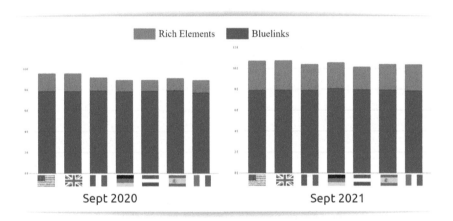

It's apparent: Rich Elements are a "must have" for any Brand SERP, and by actively managing and optimising Rich Elements, you can gain an advantage over your competitors.

Twitter Boxes

Twitter Boxes are arguably the best Rich Element to generate for your Brand SERP because they appear near the top and you directly control the content. Your original tweets feed directly into

Google and are automatically presented as Rich Elements on your Brand SERP. Google fills your Twitter Boxes with the most recent live tweets from your profile. While this can certainly impress existing customers and prospects, triggering the boxes requires a solid Twitter strategy, so you will also be reaching a larger audience in the process. It's a win-win approach to strengthening your online brand.

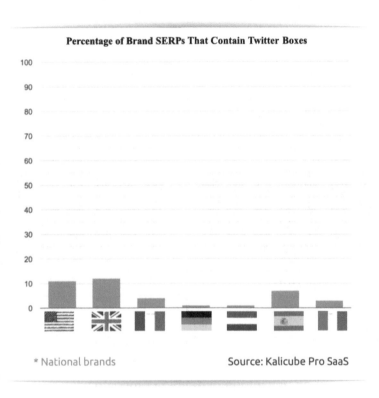

Relatively few brands have Twitter Boxes on their Brand SERPs, which is a serious "miss" on their part. They are both failing to utilize an impressive Rich Element and neglecting their Twitter strategy—a lose-lose situation!

There's no one-size-fits-all timeline for triggering Twitter Boxes on your Brand SERP; it depends on your tweeting habits, audience participation, and interaction with peers and influencers. Try to tweet 1-4 times a day, every day, with valuable content that gets engagement from relevant people and companies on Twitter. Your Twitter profile will gradually rank higher and higher on your Brand SERP over a month or two. When it appears as the second result, then you are getting close and a Twitter Box Rich Element should activate after another one to two months.

To guarantee success when tweeting, be sure to:

- Create relevant content that supports your brand message
- Use appropriate hashtags
- Tag relevant people and companies
- Use images and videos extensively

Image Boxes

If you agree with the adage that "a picture is worth a thousand words," then you'll want to have Image Boxes on your Brand SERP. Visuals not only draw the user's attention, but they can communicate your brand message at a glance. As an added bonus, Image Boxes are usually the easiest Rich Element to get.

The strategy is simple—you want to communicate your brand message using a great visual image. Every piece of content you publish should feature a quality image, whether it's on your website, a social media platform, or a third-party site.

Be strategic and consistent in your selection, though; you don't want to end up with half a dozen disjointed photos that fail to convey a unified message on your Brand SERP. Instead, consider how each image fits into the wider bouquet of your brand message. Circulate a carefully-selected dozen or so images around the web (on your site, social media platforms, and third-party sites). Google will choose images for your Brand SERP that are frequently associated with your brand and appear on multiple relevant sources. The variety of sources indicates to Google the importance of these images to you and your audience, which increases the chances of triggering Image Boxes on your Brand SERP. The consistency of the images across those sources will vastly increase the probability that Google will show the images *you* chose. Without consistency, Google could display any photo associated with your brand and rob you of any control.

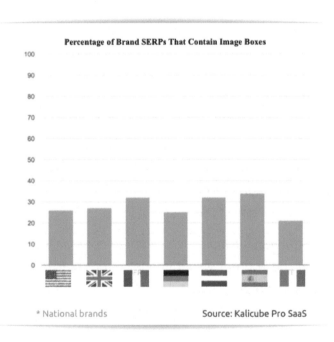

Percentage of Brand SERPs That Contain Image Boxes

* National brands   Source: Kalicube Pro SaaS

The Fundamentals of Brand SERPs for Business

Generating Successful Rich Elements

Twitter Boxes

- Consistently create posts and content.
  - ◊ Post relevant content, interact with reputable entities, and use multimedia elements to support your message.
- Engage your audience and related businesses.
- Showcase your brand name and message with your Twitter handle and profile description.

Image Boxes

- Follow basic image SEO practices.[1]
- Circulate about a dozen photos around your digital ecosystem.
- Ensure that the images you select
  - 1: Relate to your brand and its message.
  - 2: Are original.
  - 3: Don't infringe on any copyright restrictions.

Video Boxes

- Create videos that offer value to your audience and are related to your brand message.
- Post them on appropriate platforms. Although YouTube dominates, other platforms such as Vimeo, Facebook, Twitter, etc. also contribute.
- Encourage user engagement with your videos to trigger them on your Brand SERP.

---

1   For the comprehensive list, "The 10 Rules of Image SEO for Image Carousels," navigate to Kalicube.com.

PAA Panels

- Address the basic questions about your business on your website.
  - ◊ This provides Google with authoritative answers to use in the PAA panels for user questions.

- Answer questions around your core topics and prove you're a respected authority by building relationships with reputable sites and businesses.
  - ◊ Google will process these connections and will become more likely to include *your* answers for PAA panels.

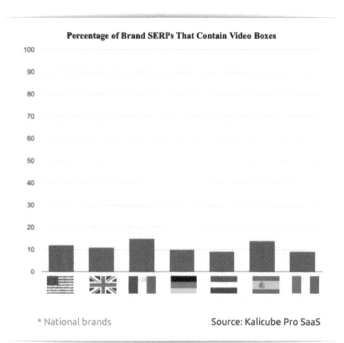

Percentage of Brand SERPs That Contain Video Boxes

* National brands   Source: Kalicube Pro SaaS

Video Boxes

Video Boxes also make great Rich Elements because they combine visuals with text on the Brand SERP, which offers an additional opening to communicate your brand message. Furthermore, video is an increasingly popular content format with users worldwide, and since Google knows this, it is keen to show relevant videos on Brand SERPs. Google actively seeks video content, so triggering Video Boxes is relatively straightforward: all you need to do is provide videos about your brand and industry that are genuinely relevant and helpful to your audience.

If you're stuck using a smartphone or cheap camera, don't worry—Google doesn't penalize videos for poor quality. Your audience might, but it's up to you to make the video beneficial and worth their time. Videos that offer real value to your audience, present applicable insights, and answer relevant questions will compensate for poor technical quality. However, you should always make the highest-quality videos you can—smartphones have amazing video and sound recording capabilities, so there really isn't an excuse for poor quality videos.

For any new content to rank on your Brand SERP, it needs to provide more value to your audience than the results currently ranking.

Videos take more time and resources to produce than written content, but they have multiple advantages.

1. Users love them.

2. Google prioritises them.

3. You can repurpose your videos into different formats across multiple platforms.

Ideally, since videos are a great format for your content strategy, you will build up a meaningful video production strategy and incorporate brand-relevant videos into it. For those videos you want to see in your Video Boxes, be sure to tie in your brand to the topic being discussed and include your brand name in the title. While it shouldn't be a sales call, the video shouldn't feel "random." Once again, it can take time for Google to understand that your videos are relevant enough to be included on your Brand SERP.

For any new content to rank on your Brand SERP, it needs to provide more value to your audience than the results currently ranking. This rule can apply to *everything* related to Brand SERP! As always, engagement, a uniform brand message, and consistent posting are key to getting your videos incorporated as a Rich Element on your Brand SERP.

Creating a High-Value Video

- Instructional how-tos: covers multiple audiences and can rank well for a wide range of questions outside Brand SERPs.

- Interviews: associates your brand with an authority or celebrity.

- Client stories: shares personal experiences of how your company has helped clients.

- Webinar: discusses relevant topics with experts where the content brings value to the audience.

- Reporting: describes your brand's purpose or news surrounding your brand, ideally reported from others (DIY is okay, but make sure it reflects well on your brand image).

- Conferences: displays a conference where you act as a sponsor, an exhibitor, or participant representing your brand.

- Client support videos: demonstrates value to existing clients.

People Also Ask (PAA) Panels

Not only are PAA panels incredibly common, but their presence is increasing fast. In late 2020, 30% of Brand SERPs had them, and a year later, this figure had risen to over 50% ("Kalicube Pro"). PAA boxes suggest and answer commonly asked user questions. In the context of Brand SERPs, the questions are about the searched brand, which vastly expands the opportunity for users to research a company directly on Google's platform without clicking through to sites. And since your audience is increasingly staying on Google to research your brand, you need to provide those answers on Google's SERP.

But who provides the answers to these questions? It's a logical assumption to think the answers come from the brands themselves, but this is not the case. Less than 25% of the PAA questions on Brand SERPs are answered by the brand owners ("Kalicube Pro"). The rest are answered by random forums, news sites, B2B sites, or (worst-case scenario) competitors. Given how users frequently consult PAA panels and place trust in the answers, PAA panels are a top priority as a Brand SERP Rich Element.

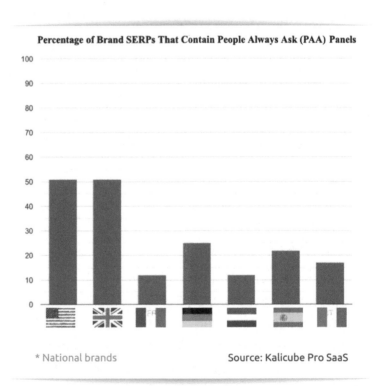

Percentage of Brand SERPs That Contain People Always Ask (PAA) Panels

* National brands   Source: Kalicube Pro SaaS

If you don't answer the questions about your business, a third-party website will, and there's no guarantee that those answers will be factual, complete, or unbiased. You can't risk users seeing an imperfect representation of your brand message and services. So few PAA are answered by the brands themselves simply because the brands don't provide clear answers for Google to use. In most cases, Google wants to provide answers "straight from the horse's mouth," but it can't! Google aims to produce clear, concise, and accurate answers, so you must ensure your website supplies them.

Here are two examples of prominent companies within a PAA panel. Ikea has answered the question on their own site, so Google is using their response. On the flip side, Jeep hasn't provided a suitable answer to a user's question, so Google is using another source, which is a missed shot for Jeep.

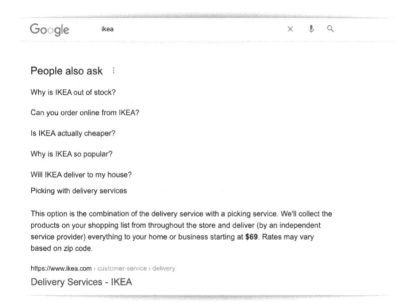

To not miss these golden opportunities to answer potential client questions, develop the FAQ section on your website in an easily digestible way. Then, you increase the chance of Google selecting your answers. As you build your FAQ pages, compose brief 100-300 word answers to the questions your audience asks. Each question should be on a dedicated page—this is easier for Google to deal with and also a better user experience for your audience, which is the ultimate goal for any business. Make sure not only to include but prioritize the questions on your Brand SERP.

General Advice on Rich Elements

As you start looking to trigger and optimise Rich Elements on your Brand SERP, remember that most of the elements will contain content from other platforms associated with your brand. So your strategy must include maintaining and optimising content about your

The Fundamentals of Brand SERPs for Business

brand on multiple platforms. If you consistently create engaging and audience-centric content about your brand, more Rich Elements will naturally appear on your Brand SERP. Google *wants* to show amazing, relevant content on your Brand SERP, and it tends to prioritise multimedia results. In addition, your online audience also wants rich, immersive content centered around your brand. Simply put, the more you create relevant, multimedia content, the better off you'll be from every perspective.

Rich Elements are the single most valuable strategy for developing a distinctive and impressive Brand SERP.

Multimedia content offers unique benefits because it's quick and easy to consume, it provides digestible information, and it grabs the audience's attention. For more information on creating and presenting content that appeals to Google's algorithm, please refer to the chapter on SEO tactics (*Chapter Eight*) and the relevant Kalicube course ("Triggering and Optimising Rich Elements").

Rich Elements are the single most valuable strategy for developing a distinctive and impressive Brand SERP. They even come with a simple yet powerful bonus; by focusing your online strategy on this easy "win," you're also improving your digital ecosystem and audience outreach at the same time.

To know if your efforts are on the right track, look at your Brand SERP. The more multimedia content Google shows, the more well-developed and powerful your online content strategy is. Once you've generated enough "noise" online, your brand may be given a Knowledge Panel, which is arguably the final seal of Google's approval of your brand.

CHAPTER SEVEN

Managing Knowledge Panels

Google's Knowledge Panels are the ultimate Rich Element—they add credibility to your brand, demonstrate Google's stamp of approval, and offer users a convenient package of information on your brand.

Google Knowledge Panel ⋖

Knowledge panels are **information boxes that appear on Google** when you search for entities (people, places, organizations, things) that are in the Knowledge Graph. They are meant to help you get a quick snapshot of information on a topic based on Google's understanding of available content on the web.

https://support.google.com › knowledgepanel ›
About knowledge panels - Google Support

Essentially, Knowledge Panels are representations of Google's understanding of the world, including its understanding of your brand.

A Knowledge Panel will often appear on the right-hand side of search results on desktop when you search for an entity: people, places, organisations, podcasts, music groups, films, TV series, etc. In short, any searchable "thing." This panel contains information Google considers to be factual in response to a user's search query. Essentially, Knowledge Panels are representations of Google's understanding of the world, including its understanding of your brand.

It is fundamentally important that Google has its facts straight so it can build your Brand SERP to accurately depict who you are, what you do, and what audience you serve. An optimised Knowledge Panel of your brand will prompt a more beneficial Brand SERP. Therefore, having an accurate and helpful Knowledge Panel is an absolute must-have for your brand.

Google's Knowledge Panel gathers fragments of information from a wide range of trusted and authoritative online sources. This is done using an algorithm to review and evaluate human-curated information (Wikipedia, Google Books, etc.) and other content found by GoogleBot. The information is cross-referenced using trusted sources to try to ensure its accuracy. Google's ultimate goal is to compile truthful and accurate information and present it in a useful way for its users.

You have partial control over what your audience sees in the Knowledge Panel when they Google your brand name. The process is simple: as you optimise your Brand SERP, you will correct the

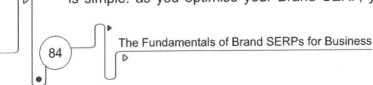

The Fundamentals of Brand SERPs for Business

most influential information about your brand. This will naturally create a better understanding for Google and build confidence in its understanding. Eventually, Google will trigger a Knowledge Panel that accurately reflects your brand (or ensure an existing Knowledge Panel portrays accurate information over time).

An accurate and well-documented Knowledge Panel is a strong indication that Google understands who you are, what you do, and who your audience is. That makes for a more representative Brand SERP, better SEO performances, and (the cherry on the cake) it increases credibility to prospective clients. Knowledge Panels are becoming a common fixture for branded queries, so not having one can hurt your business since it may discourage prospects and returning customers.

Credibility will help build and stabilise your Knowledge Panel. Google calls this EAT: Expertise, Authoritativeness, and Trustworthiness. Demonstrating to Google that your brand is respected and in demand by your peers and your audience is essential to securing a Knowledge Panel. So, you need to generate a buzz in your peer community and with your audience. You can reinforce this curated buzz by including links from your site to the third-party content that mentions your brand. Then, Google is sure to understand that all of the media attention is, indeed, about you, and thereby improve your E-A-T credentials. This positive buzz around your brand will not only help Google recognise your relevancy, but it will also improve its understanding and confidence in that understanding—not to mention the publicity will increase brand awareness in your target audience and potentially increase sales. There's another big bonus to remember: a better E-A-T score will be a significant help to your overall SEO strategy.

EAT at Google

This acronym is related to how Google measures credibility.

Expertise: Is the information accurate? Is the writer or brand a credible source for writing about the topic?

Authoritativeness: Is the author well-respected in their field? Is the brand widely recognized in the industry? Is the content referred to elsewhere on the web by other reputable and authoritative websites, brands, and people?

Trustworthiness: Does the brand and writer have a good reputation, and does the audience trust them?

Google judges credibility, or "EAT," at three levels: the content, the author, and the publisher. As you develop your Brand SERP, make sure you pass the "EAT" test and that any businesses or sites you cultivate a relationship with also meet these standards.

The three determining factors for your Knowledge Panel are:

1. Google's understanding of who you are

2. Google's confidence in its understanding

3. The probability that the user's search query refers to a specific entity and that the Knowledge Panel is therefore helpful to the user

Building a diverse and active digital ecosystem is essential for building accurate brand understanding, confidence, and awareness. This "winning" combination is what will ultimately generate a Knowledge Panel for your brand.

Knowledge Panel Composition

Knowledge Panels display brief summaries about searched-for entities. Take the Knowledge Panel of Leonardo Da Vinci as an example.

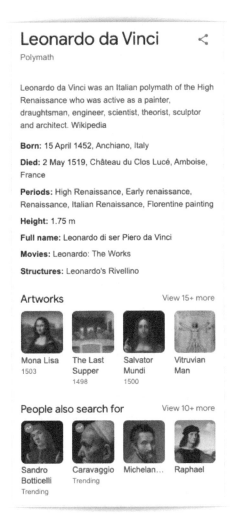

Google uses a vast number of sources to verify Da Vinci's artistic contributions and it recognises other information as facts, such as his birth date. Google is able to associate Da Vinci with some of his artworks, and also identifies him as a 15th century Italian painter connected to Michelangelo by these attributes. In the Knowledge Panel, Google links those entities and facts together to create connections, much like the human brain does. As a result, Google can display a summary of the most useful information concerning Leonardo Da Vinci, while allowing users to find other related information about him with a single click. Now imagine what a Knowledge Panel would look like for *your* brand and how it might make a difference to your audience.

A Brand SERP that features a rich and accurate Knowledge Panel allows users to understand your brand, mission, and product/service with one search—a huge win for your digital strategy.

Knowledge Panels are a growing SERP element in Google's world. There is a lot to understand about them, but the core idea is relatively straightforward: Knowledge Panels provide a quick summary of your brand in one panel. Thus, they aid Google's goal of displaying an unbiased overview of your brand, while also answering basic user questions and eliminating the need to visit multiple sites for information about you. As with every strategy discussed in this book, SEO techniques will amplify the benefits of Knowledge Panels. When you apply basic SEO techniques to manage your brand's Knowledge Panel, you ensure the information Google provides in these "information boxes" is accurate and helpful to your audience.

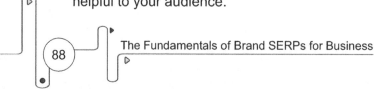

A Brand SERP that features a rich and accurate Knowledge Panel allows users to understand your brand, mission, and product/service with one search—a huge win for your digital strategy.

Knowledge Panels are one of the most complex and difficult aspects of Brand SERP optimisation, and the subject requires a book all of its own (which I'll be writing in 2022). This chapter provides a basic overview of what they are and why they are vital for your brand.

Below, I've included the outline of my condensed, three-step process for managing your Knowledge Panel. To dig deeper, please visit the link at the end of the summary and get started on your journey to understanding how Knowledge Panels work and what you can do to manage yours. Or, you can wait for my next book to learn more about Knowledge Panels, which are *truly simple, incredibly effective, and astonishingly powerful.*

Summary of Acquiring a Knowledge Panel

- Identify the Entity Home
  - ◊ This is the one, single webpage where an entity "lives" online.
  - ◊ You need to make it the go-to place for Google to find information about your company.
  - ◊ The page should be on your own website.
- Set Out the Facts
  - ◊ State the facts about your brand in a clear description.
  - ◊ Organise this information using informative headings/subheadings.
  - ◊ Add Organisation Schema.org markup, which offers the best way for you to communicate information about your brand in Google's "native language."
- Provide Corroboration
  - ◊ Identify the authoritative sources that confirm the facts about you.
  - ◊ Signpost (link out to) those sources from your Entity Home.
  - ◊ Correct all the facts and info on those sources so they confirm what you say on the Entity Home.
  - ◊ Where possible, add a link back from those sources to your Entity Home.

For more information on Knowledge Panels, visit

https://kalicube.com/faq/knowledge-panels/knowledge-panel-definition/

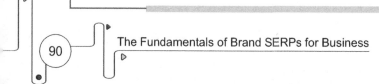

CHAPTER EIGHT

SEO Tactics, Techniques, and Strategies

Search Engine Optimisation (SEO) tactics are the key tools on your Brand SERP belt and the foundation of the wider digital strategy for your brand. Because they are "good housekeeping" for online content and reputation, consistently applying SEO techniques and strategies will vastly improve your brand's digital presence, starting (of course) with your Brand SERP. Any improvements you make to your Brand SERP will improve your overall digital presence, online reputation, content marketing efforts, SEO, and by extension, your sales too. It seems too good to be true, but the cumulation of many small improvements offers big wins for you across the board long term. Luckily, the majority of the SEO tactics you'll need are non-technical, simple, and easy to implement.

The importance of SEO to any brand strategy cannot be emphasised enough, as evident in the numerous online articles covering SEO techniques, tactics, and strategies. But not all of these articles effectively break down the SEO approach, few make SEO accessible to non-technical people and even fewer consider the benefits beyond ranking on Google and Bing.

If you approach SEO from a Brand SERP perspective, you can be just as effective and get a better ROI with very little need for a technical department.[1] In short, you can flip focus and resources from 20% content and 80% technical to 20% technical and 80% content. By understanding SEO from a Brand SERP perspective, you can vastly reduce your reliance on the technical aspects and prioritise engaging your audience with the content you create. Of course, you still need the technical foundation (which I describe briefly later in this chapter), but you can focus more resources on creating great content for your audience so your business can drive sales. Prioritising the customer with this approach is just common sense in business. Whatever your objective, whether it's internet fame or acquiring a steady stream of clients, practical, non-technical SEO tactics should absolutely be a part of your daily plug and chug.

Revisit the Basic Motive

My approach to SEO is straightforward—it's packaging your content to help Google perform and achieve its goals. Google's users are (explicitly or implicitly) searching for an answer to a question or problem, so Google's ultimate aim is to provide its users with the most effective and efficient answer or solution. And just like any business, Google prioritises customer satisfaction and will recommend you as the solution only when it is convinced you can satisfy its user.

---

1   ROI: Return on Investment

The Fundamentals of Brand SERPs for Business

Google's understanding and perception of your brand is central to your Brand SERP and also to your overall SEO strategy. For every Google search where your brand appears, it synthesises your content and frames the information within its understanding of your brand.

If you begin viewing each and every Google SERP as a product and package your content so it can contribute to that product, then your overall SEO strategy will shift. You will have a more realistic, less technical, marketing-focused approach to SEO that will ultimately be more successful.

So Google's understanding of your brand—who you are, what you do, and which audience you serve—is key. And your Brand SERP is an easy-to-read reflection of Google's understanding of your brand, your content, and your relationship with your audience. You truly are "winning the game" when your Brand SERP is an accurate reflection of you, projects the brand message you want, and contains content that is engaging your audience to the point where they become brand advocates.

There are three crucial pillars for effective SEO:

1. Understanding

   ◊ How well does Google understand who you are, what you offer, and who your audience is?

     ▪ Once Google understands you and which audience you serve, the algorithms can start offering your content as a solution to the subsection of its users who are your audience.

2. Credibility

   ◊ Is Google confident that your business is superior to your competition?

     ▪ After you've established credibility (EAT), you will beat your competition as the best candidate as a solution to the user's search query.

3. Suitability

   ◊ Is your content a good fit for the Google SERP "product"?

     ▪ Google's ultimate aim (its product) is to help its users effectively find the best solutions to the problems they express with a search query. Essentially, your goal becomes helping Google achieve *its* goal, which is helping its users achieve *their* goals.

If you begin viewing each and every Google SERP as a product and package your content so it can contribute to that product, then your overall SEO strategy will shift. You will have a more realistic, less technical, marketing-focused approach to SEO that will ultimately be more successful.

You need to understand and apply this approach and use SEO techniques in order to optimise your Brand SERP and that, in turn, will help your overall SEO strategy. I advise all of my clients to build their online strategy from the Brand SERP outwards. Implementing effective SEO on your Brand SERP will improve the wider online impact of your brand.

The days when you could succeed in SEO with just one tactic are long gone. In the past, low-quality content could rank by having boatloads of backlinks, and well-optimised content could rank with just a few backlinks. It was a tactics-based contest. Not anymore. You need to have a strategic brand approach for SEO to deliver ROI. And your Brand SERP is the window into the effectiveness of this strategy.

The vast majority of companies and brands working on their SEO haven't laid the proper foundations. Ask yourself: "What is the core of my business? Am I performing there?" Your Brand SERP provides a simple and powerful insight into this question. If it reflects who you are and how your audience perceives you, then you are on the right track and you just need to leverage the insights your Brand SERP provides to improve your winning strategy. If not, you need to use your Brand SERP to recalibrate and improve your digital strategy, then build outwards.

The Game-Changing Hummingbird

Prior to 2013, SEO was just a numbers game. For years, Google used to evaluate the number and ratio of words, factor in the number and quality of inbound links, and then calculate a ranking based on a word-and-link count. The rudimentary system made it easy for smart marketers and business owners to find tricks and tactics to manipulate Google.

That is no longer the case. In 2013, Google released the "Hummingbird" update. With Hummingbird, Google started to understand the world in a manner similar to the human brain; it analyses things (entities) such as companies and understands them through their relationship to other entities, such as products and offers. So now, instead of counting links and words, Google analyses the pieces—it evaluates its understanding of your business and your offers, much like a human being would. Google "intelligently" evaluates the solution you can provide and calculates the match between your solution and the needs of the person, and the quality of your solution compared to your competition.

With this new approach, quality offers with genuine value to Google's users are increasingly dominating the results. In order to be part of this revolution, you need to help Google better understand your brand, your content, and your offers by employing SEO techniques on your content.

The Foundational Techniques

The first, and most important, technique is clear copywriting. Google understands entities and relationships between them, much like we humans do. The foundation of this is using Subject-Verb-Object—grammar everyone learns in school. Google calls this a semantic triple, which may sound complicated, but it is actually just standard sentence composition. Google's algorithm is looking for the "subject verb object" within your content. Basically, the verb should demonstrate the relationship between the subject (the primary entity) and the object (the other entity), and the three parts should be close together so the machine doesn't get confused. This means writing "Adidas makes shoes" rather than "Adidas, the German company founded in 1949, makes shoes."

The Fundamentals of Brand SERPs for Business

Naturally, there's a balance between writing compelling copy that appeals to customers and using transparent language to inform Google. Your writing should be clear and use precise verbs to describe the relationships between identifiable entities. Google is trying to understand who you are and what you have to offer its user; a semantic triple simplifies its processing of this information. With clear copywriting, Google will be able to connect the entities correctly in its "mind" and understand the meaning of the text, and you should still be able to keep the content attractive to your site visitors.

The trick is to write clear content for Google to easily process without weighing down the language so much that your audience no longer enjoys it. As such, ensure you "sandwich" semantic triples between more attractive and compelling sentences. Semantic triples may improve Google's understanding of your content, but your audience will not appreciate paragraphs solely composed of short, abrupt sentences.

Another powerful writing technique is mastering the use of headings. Used properly, they are helpful to users and instructive to Google about the written content on your page. Be sure to include only one H1 (primary title), which functions as a short description of the overall topic of the page. Then you'll have one or more secondary headings (H2) used to divide the content into subtopics. Each should briefly and clearly describe what information the user (and Google) will find in the subsequent paragraphs. Think of it like a book: the H1 is the front-cover title of the book and each H2 is a chapter title. The user (and Google) should be able to skim through the headings and immediately understand what the page is all about and which section they should refer to for any specific questions.

Multimedia plays into this more than you perhaps realise. Google has invested vast resources analysing images and videos to help it understand the world. Semantic triples in your written content are great. Providing supporting rich media is critical.

Plain written content is not enough anymore; the results need to be supported with multimedia for Google and your audience to find your content relevant and valuable. Mixed media, such as images, videos, and audio, are an effective way to communicate with the audience *and* they bring immense added value to your Brand SERP too. This ties back to the idea of replacing results on your Brand SERP page with rich results. Multimedia results are not only more impressive and convincing for your audience, but they push other, less relevant links down on the page. And because they are large, they often reduce the total number of results shown on the first page.

When adding multimedia elements such as images to your content, make sure to enter descriptive alt tags (the HTML explanatory code for a graphic) and use a clear file name. The site visitor won't see either, but these tags will help Google understand the contents of your multimedia elements and encourage it to add Rich Elements to your Brand SERP. Improving your Brand SERP is about optimising every piece of content about and around your brand using every possible technique available to you, no matter how basic.

On the technical side of SEO for your Brand SERP, all of the content needs to be "crawlable." Basically, Google needs permission to visit and digest your content without being blocked by security rules. Crawlability also refers to ensuring that there is a discernible path to each page from the homepage. Header menus, footers, links in your web pages, including your homepage, significantly improve Google's maneuverability, which will ultimately improve your SEO.

Your website pages need to be fast-loading, mobile-friendly, and organised in blocks to be easy to digest for Google. Pages should ideally load in under two seconds for your average 3G connection. Google is all about user satisfaction, and site users are going to be frustrated if they have to wait too long for content. Google measures the speed of every page and then uses the data to influence your ranking. Although page speed is important in SEO, it is less important for Brand SERPs and should not come at the expense of crawlability, mobile friendliness, organising content in blocks, and the quality of the content itself.

A mobile-friendly website means that the design, images, videos, etc. display correctly and are ergonomic on the smaller screen of a mobile device (phone or tablet). Think about some of the sites you frequently visit; if you are using a mobile device, you'll either have an ergonomic display right off the bat or be prompted to move to the company's dedicated mobile app or mobile site. These are all ways companies can provide a great experience for their users on mobile. Google is actively checking to see if a site's mobile version satisfies customers. When the site falls short, it is at a distinct disadvantage: Google doesn't want to send its users to a site with second-rate experience on mobile.

Another important SEO factor is the visual appeal of the content. Is it attractive? Readable? Did you include multimedia elements? It might sound strange, but Google has technology that allows the machine to visualise your page, meaning its algorithms judge these aspects too. These components improve your SEO "score" and can be simple ways to improve the performance of your content on Google for both your Brand SERP and your wider SEO strategy.

When organising the content, you want the information to be broken into digestible blocks or "chunks." When your content has clear, identifiable blocks, such as paragraphs or sections, then Google can more easily analyse the page, understand the content, and (importantly) determine the key points. Google takes these key points and repurposes them in the SERP in many ways: Knowledge Panel descriptions, Featured Snippets, People Also Ask panel, thumbnail images, sitelinks, and many more. Great "content chunking" helps Google help its users, which means you win too.

Here's some content Google has extracted from the middle of a well-chunked page and used on a SERP:

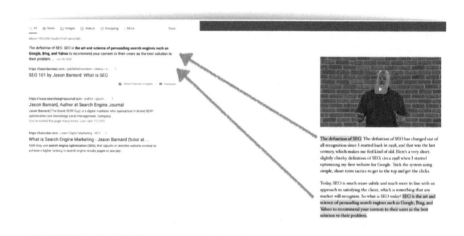

Writing for Online Content

The writing style for online content is very different from a letter or this book. As you write the content for your brand, be clear and concise, explain who you are, your products/services, and why a user should select your business.

Keep the writing intelligible; you don't need to "dumb it down" for users, but you also aren't trying to win any creative writing contests here. The end goal is to get your brand message across to your audience and Google effectively. Accessible writing also makes the content more visually appealing, especially when combined with well-organised chunks. Nobody wants to visit a site and be met with a giant block of text they'll have to to find the key information.

Direct language also ensures that sentences still make sense when taken out of the context of your web page. When Google grabs a chunk of your content to answer a user's query, the content needs to make sense in the context of Google's SERP. It needs to stand alone and convey information without the user navigating to visit your site. Does your content pass this test?

You need Google to understand your content, but you want to maintain balance so your writing still appeals to the reader, who is, after all, the most important consumer. Users can tell superficial writing from genuine content, so be sincere. Try to include their point of view and speak to the person beyond the screen. Many brands write from their own perspective with an inside view, and they forget that the people consuming the content are perhaps meeting the business for the first time. Don't assume the reader knows you or your services, and start with a compelling introduction to your brand. As you write, focus on their viewpoint and try to create a team spirit, the idea that together, you and I, can solve the problem you're facing.

Always remember the fundamental rules for establishing an online presence: *Be relevant. Provide valuable content. Stay on topic.*

Tactics that Amplify Your Digital Signal

There's a myriad of other tactics for improving your SEO and Brand SERP to amplify and improve your digital signal. Other tactics include internal, external, and inbound linking, fresh content, third-party corroboration, and user-generated content.

Internal linking serves as a navigation tool. Anticipate what the user will need on your site and create logical links within your pages. Think of this as creating signposts to valuable content for users in need of directions. Be sure to add links to your content only when they are relevant to the user since the primary goal is to help them.

Then, think about linking to and from results on other sites that are within your control (social media, profile pages, guest articles, reviews, etc.). These are valuable resources for your audience and they are also helpful to Google since it sees the connections between these third party sites and yours, thus solidifying its understanding of you.

In your content, you'll also want to include some relevant links to other credible sites. (But don't overdo it; one or two external links per page is usually enough).

You can achieve this in two different ways:

1. Include links to a third-party site that mentions your brand. A mention or interview on a powerful site, such as *entrepreneur.com*, is great, but don't overlook industry-specific sites. These third-party industry-specific mentions will be just as powerful for your brand because of the authority they have in your niche and the value they offer to your audience. For instance, if I'm running a dog shampooing salon in Paris, it's just as valuable, arguably more valuable, to be mentioned by *poodleparloursinparis.com*. This embedded link on your website will benefit your authority in Google's "mind," which will help your EAT, your SEO, and your Brand SERP. Relationships with relevant sites establish you as an authority in your industry and indicate to Google that your content is relevant and important to your audience.

2. Embed links to credible sources within your content, even when your brand isn't mentioned. In a discussion on SEO, you could quote and link to an article from inc.com: "SEO

is a future department of marketing that can be a make-or-break strategy for a company. SEO will increase your digital presence and acquire a larger customer base for your business." Doing this gives Google a reference to check the accuracy of what you are saying, and since inc. com is an authoritative magazine for small businesses and entrepreneurs, the link to their article will help build trust, which will improve your SEO and your overall Brand SERP.

The more you can establish respected connections and build a reputation in the industry, the better your Brand SERP will be and the more your SEO strategy will perform. These online connections are the way you can build your E-A-T (Expertise, Authoritativeness, and Trustworthiness). Google sees and understands links and mentions. The more implicit and explicit connections you have to other relevant, credible sources, the more your E-A-T will benefit. From there, there's a snowball effect of improvement, so your Brand SERP will look better and your investments in SEO will provide greater ROI.

Starting from Scratch and Growing Outwards

If you have a small online reach and few connections, the natural way to increase both is to generate fresh, relevant content that is meaningful to your peers, attractive to your industry, and engaging for your audience.

As we have seen, creating fresh content, packaging it for Google, and encouraging user participation will not only improve your Brand SERP, but will also boost your wider SEO and overall digital performance. Create a plan to add new content regularly.

It doesn't have to be every day, or even every week, but there needs to be a consistent flow of "action" on your site and your preferred social channels. Consistent content production strengthens Google's trust in your brand while also increasing audience loyalty and engagement. It's a win-win.

Some content you create will be everlasting, as the basic information about your company won't change very much over the years. An article or video about the fundamentals of your industry won't significantly change either. Even so, updating it from time to time (perhaps once a year) clearly indicates to Google that the information is still accurate and relevant. Other content is short term and will be relevant and helpful for a few days, weeks, or months. Both types of content are needed for your audience and Google.

Once you have a consistent content routine, it is a great idea to post links to your new content on your social media accounts. The links will help Google find the content and see that it is relevant and valuable to your audience. Google will then improve its understanding, build its confidence in you as a brand, and improve your Brand SERP. It will also encourage your social media followers to visit, or revisit, your site, which is a non-negligible "bonus." It's another win-win.

It is incredibly important to link your social media profiles to your site and link your site to your social media profiles. Two-way linking is vital for Google to be confident that these are indeed your social media profiles. Once Google is confident, it will push your relevant social media content higher up your Brand SERP, and as we saw in a previous chapter, this activity will help push those social profiles up your Brand SERP and trigger those Rich Elements.

Whether on social media, on third-party sites, or on your own site, your content should be attractive and valuable to your audience. This applies to written content and multimedia elements embedded in your content, as well as any other ways your brand communicates with your audience online.

You also need to look at what your audience is saying. What your audience says about you online is even more important than what you say about yourself. Encourage clients and peers to speak positively about you on social media, forums, and their own sites. Reviews in particular are powerful, especially on independent third-party sites. If you feel that encouraging reviews from your customers or feedback from your peers is a gamble, then think about why this might be. If you aren't confident enough in your products and services to expect positive feedback, then start by improving them to the point where you are confident that over 80% of feedback will be positive. Only then should you start actively encouraging audience feedback on social media, in articles, and through reviews.

Because the feedback from your clients, partners, and peers is impartial, it is a very strong quality signal to Google and a major contributor to your E-A-T, not to mention an incredibly powerful encouragement for your prospective clients. And, of course, content that contains impartial feedback from your audience will also be a good candidate for your Brand SERP.

This chapter is a little lengthy because SEO techniques are the driving force behind your ability to design the anatomy of your "Google Business Card." It's no exaggeration to say that SEO techniques are the means by which you communicate with Google and educate it about your brand.

But bear in mind they are just one part of your overall Brand SERP strategy. Google heavily depends on the content and quality signals across your entire digital ecosystem: your site, social media platforms, third-party mentions, content you create, content you distribute, audience engagement, feedback, reviews, etc. In short, this means *everything available online*. Google analyses and processes everything you do online and everything surrounding your brand. This means all of your brand's actions and audience feedback affect Google's understanding of your brand and its credibility. SEO techniques are a way to package all of this for Google so that it understands the content and appreciates its true value, which in turn allows Google to better understand your brand and evaluate your credibility.

Even if you've worked through each technique and strategy in this book thus far, some brands require more help in order to generate organic traffic and capture audience attention. Google Ads offer an easy, cost-effective way to optimise your Brand SERP real estate and potentially gain sales.

CHAPTER NINE

Optimising Google Ads

Advertisements can be a tricky grey area in brand-building. Too few, and you'll struggle to build your client base; too many, and your brand loses the perceived esteem. In your digital marketing strategy, you have to be very strategic in choosing where to run your ads since there are an endless number of options.

Google is generally a good starting point. Remember, the people Googling your brand name are your audience. If they are using Google, then they see Google as trustworthy and authoritative. The message it projects through your Brand SERP is important to you. Google Ads appear front and center at the top of your Brand SERP, and more importantly, you control the message.

Before incorporating Google Ads into your Brand SERP strategy, it's important to have some context on how Google Ads works.

4,978,042,801

Google Searches today

view how many in 1 second

Google Search Volume (current and historical)

Growth Rate

Search Market Share

Sources and References

Consider how many times a day people visit Google to verify a quick fact, navigate to a website, conduct intensive research, or go shopping. Google processes several billion searches every day. The running count on this screenshot never paused for a single second; people were continuously searching on Google.[1]

Google generates income by inserting ads at the top of some search results. Between 4% and 10% of searches on Google contain ads; this depends on the country, language, and device ("Semrush"). Ads on Google searches look very similar to organic search results, as you can see here:

---

1   The photo was taken at 2:20pm US-EST on October 29, 2021.

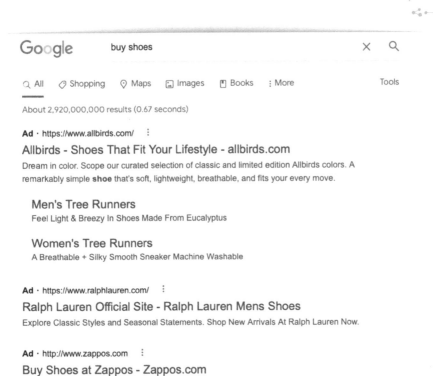

Google   buy shoes   × 🔍

🔍 All   ⊘ Shopping   📍 Maps   🖻 Images   📖 Books   ⋮ More   Tools

About 2,920,000,000 results (0.67 seconds)

Ad · https://www.allbirds.com/ ⋮
Allbirds - Shoes That Fit Your Lifestyle - allbirds.com
Dream in color. Scope our curated selection of classic and limited edition Allbirds colors. A
remarkably simple **shoe** that's soft, lightweight, breathable, and fits your every move.

Men's Tree Runners
Feel Light & Breezy In Shoes Made From Eucalyptus

Women's Tree Runners
A Breathable + Silky Smooth Sneaker Machine Washable

Ad · https://www.ralphlauren.com/ ⋮
Ralph Lauren Official Site - Ralph Lauren Mens Shoes
Explore Classic Styles and Seasonal Statements. Shop New Arrivals At Ralph Lauren Now.

Ad · http://www.zappos.com ⋮
Buy Shoes at Zappos - Zappos.com
Free Shipping & Free 365 Day Return Huge Selection of **Shoes**! Nike. Birkenstock. Born.

Google only charges the advertiser if the user clicks on the ad, which makes it an attractive form of online advertising. This is called "Pay Per Click."

You have probably realised that, as an advertiser, this is an opportunity to jump the queue, get your offers to the top of Google's search results, and generate organic traffic simply by paying Google. But using this strategy to get your ad to the top of Google is not as easy or straightforward as you might think. For popular search queries, a lot of companies are vying to get the top position on the search results through Google Ads. Google uses a complex algorithm to decide which ones to show and how much to charge for each click. The algorithm judges the quality of the advertisements, their relevance to the search query, and the quality of the site behind the ad. It selects the ones most likely to get a click from the user and therefore generate revenue for Google.

How Can You "Score" an Ad?

Google Ads is a bidding system. Advertisers bid against each other to appear on the search queries they are interested in. You might think the advertiser who pays the most will always win, but this is not necessarily true. The algorithm uses Google Ads Quality Score to evaluate which ads appear at the top of the SERP and also how much the advertiser will pay for a click. The algorithm aims to drive revenue for Google, but not at the expense of ruining the search results page for the user. This is where Quality Score comes into play. The algorithm uses Quality Score to ensure it only retains ads that are relevant and helpful to its users.

But Google goes further than this. It rewards advertisers who produce ads that *truly* satisfy its users by applying lower cost per click to ads with a higher Quality Score. The higher the Quality Score, the less Google will charge for the click on the ad. It sounds strange, but the system maintains a balance where all three parties are happy: advertisers, Google's users, and (of course) Google.

The Google Ads algorithm calculates Quality Score on a scale of 1 to 10. With a score of 10 for an ad, the advertiser will pay significantly less for a click on their ad than an advertiser who produces an ad with a Quality Score of 5. Obviously the ratios change depending on markets, competition, and algorithm updates, but to give you an idea, an advertiser with a Quality Score of 10 might pay 10x less than an advertiser who produces an ad with a Quality Score of 1.

Quality Score is measured according to three factors:

1. Ad relevance for the user

2. Expected click-through rate (CTR)

3. Landing page experience

The details of how the algorithm behind Google Ads actually functions is a mystery, much like the search (SEO) algorithm. We know the levers to pull to get profitable results, but Google keeps the behind-curtain workings obscure. It's like completing a puzzle in the dark—you can recognize some of the pieces and put them together, but you can't see what the pieces look like. You have to multitask here: work from the outside to make the Google Ads perform for your business, while also satisfying Google and its users. Quality Score is the measurement we can see, understand, and actively manage, so improving its three factors will optimise your Google Ads campaigns.

Ad Relevance

If a user searches for "buy red shoes" and an advertiser is bidding on this search result with an ad offering blue hats, Google will score the ad very low for relevance since the result does not provide a relevant solution to the search query. Google will charge an advertiser more if they place an ad for hats on a search for shoes.

Expected Click-Through Rate

This factor is calculated according to how well the ad is written. An ad will be attributed a high Quality Score if it presents an attractive offer to the user, has great copywriting, and uses tone and vocabulary to entice a user to click on the ad. Subsequently, an advertiser will pay less if their ad contains great copywriting and their offer is attractive and well-presented.

Landing Page Experience

When analysing the landing page experience for users, the algorithm looks at what happens after the user has clicked on the ad. Google asks itself several questions: does the page actually offer what is promised in the ad? Is the web page user-friendly? An advertiser will pay less if Google sees that their page loads quickly, has an appropriate offer, is well-presented, and solves its user's problem efficiently.

Once you understand the three factors that influence high Quality Scores and drive low cost per click, solving the Google Ads "puzzle" is certainly doable.

Brand SERPs and Google Ads

When it comes to Brand SERPs and Google Ads, a couple of questions immediately spring to mind. Why would I place an ad on my own brand name? If I do, how can I ensure I get a high Quality Score and keep costs down?

Not every brand needs to bid on their own brand name. Sometimes competitors will bid on your brand name and their ads will appear at the top of your Brand SERP. When this happens, you will definitely want to act and create a Google Ads campaign of your own to get them off your Brand SERP.

If your competitors never appear in the paid results on your Brand SERP, then your own website will appear at the top, and you have no obvious need to consider Google Ads for your brand name. However, before rejecting Google Ads out of hand, consider that a well-optimised branded ad campaign costs little (starting at a few cents per click) and allows you to dominate the top positions of your Brand SERP with a message *you* control.

For a search involving your exact brand term, you will generally score high for all three Quality Score factors with absolutely no effort. Even so, there are many techniques to improve each factor further and boost your Quality Score to significantly reduce cost. By improving each of the components, my clients often reduce their cost per click by 30% or more.

My clients also gain more control of their Brand SERP. When you have an ad at the top, especially a rich ad like Hubspot's below, you control significantly more real estate on your Brand SERP, which is ideal for Brand SERP optimisation. As you can see, HubSpot controls the SERP real estate for everything the user sees when the page initially loads (above the fold):

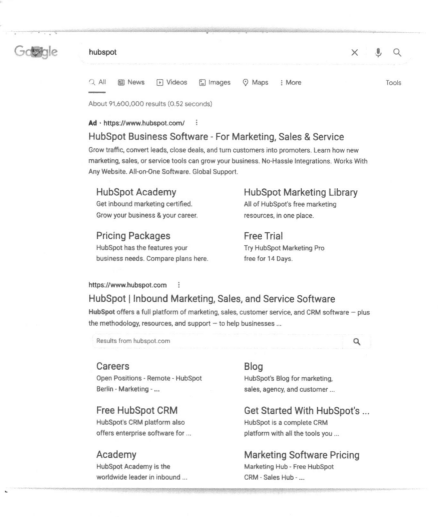

This direct control is a crucial part in HubSpot's marketing strategy, and with their combination of an ad and Rich Sitelinks, HubSpot is significantly reducing any possible "leak to the competition" of their clients and prospects.

So, with or without your competitors placing ads on your Brand SERP, Google Ads may be a profitable strategy. Here's how you keep costs down.

Ad Relevance: By definition, you are the most relevant for your own brand name, so you might think there are no improvements to be made here. This is one mistake most brands make. They don't isolate their own brand name in a dedicated Google Ads campaign. When you have an ad campaign centered around your **exact** brand name, Google's algorithms better understand the relevance of the ads within the campaign and this pushes your ad relevance score upwards.

Expected Click-Through Rate: The CTR of your ad to an audience who is searching for your brand might seem inconsequential. This assumption couldn't be more wrong. Great copywriting that appeals to your audience is never a "given." A bad ad is a bad ad, even on a Brand SERP, so put in the work on your presentation.

Landing Page Experience: Once again, this may seem like a given. You certainly have an advantage over the competition since the offer you present is exactly what they are looking for. And yet, there are several levers you can use here to help you win big with your Google Ads campaign. Most brands use their homepage as the landing page, but a dedicated landing page elevates your brand to the next level.

1. You have more leeway to optimise it for the Google Ads algorithm.

2. You can make the page load faster and improve the brand message on the page.

3. You can even present attractive, dedicated special offers on the page that your audience will be unable to resist.

When implemented intelligently, all of these "bonus" benefits will increase user engagement, which is the signal the algorithm is looking at for this aspect of the Quality Score.

Advice for Specific Situations

International Campaigns: If you target several territories, then consider creating a Google Ads campaign for each. Relevancy is unlikely to be a significant lever here, but expected CTR and landing page experience certainly are. Adjustments to language, culture, and regional vocabulary are all going to help improve your expected CTR and landing page experience for each territory.

Protecting Yourself Against Ad "Theft": Your competitors are allowed to bid on your brand name and try to entice your audience with a paid result through Google Ads.

Unfortunately, by default, Google will allow competitors to use your brand name in their ad copy on your Brand SERP until the day you explicitly inform Google of your trademark claim. Make your claim on every trademarked territory with your brand name to ensure your competitors will no longer be able to use your brand name in their copywriting. If you combine this with the other strategies I mention, they will disappear from the top of your Brand SERP and stop leeching off of your good reputation.

In conclusion, Google Ads rewards advertisements with high Quality Scores by charging the advertiser less per ad click. On your own brand name, you have a significant natural advantage over your competitors, which means you have the power to push your Quality Score *way* up. And because Google Ads Quality Score

is relative, your ad successes happen at your competitor's literal expense. The ad cost works like a seesaw: the better Quality Score you have, the less you pay, and the more expensive it is for your competitor.

The Kalicube course, "The Fundamentals of Brand SERPs," offers a module on Google Ads that contains more techniques to reduce ad costs for your brand campaign.

Google's bottom line is user satisfaction, so it will only reduce their satisfaction for the "right" cost. Your competitor will have to pay this higher cost if they bid on your Brand SERP real estate. Your competitor's business is relevant to your results because your products/services are related, so Google is willing to include their ad. But you still have control here. The better you optimise your Google ad, the less likely it will be for your competitor to gain traction and appear on your Brand SERP, potentially stealing your prospects and customers from right under your nose.

Some businesses look for quick and easy shortcut solutions to generate Google Ads traffic using automated platforms. These can work well for non-brand searches, but very rarely work in the specific context of Brand SERPs. As a general rule, Google does not take kindly to cheaters, not with Google Ads or any other Brand SERP feature. You create a strong, secure digital ecosystem by investing real time and effort. Any attempt to outsmart Google endangers both your brand and reputation and allows your competition to get ahead.

CHAPTER TEN

Tactics to Avoid
and Mistakes Not to Make

The leading message of this book is that Google is your new business card, and your Brand SERP reflects the world's opinion of your brand. The most valuable aspect of a Brand SERP is its ability to emphasise your quality and credibility as a business. As long as your Brand SERP achieves this goal and benefits your brand, you have unparalleled wins with a great "Google Business Card."

But what will you do if your Brand SERP displays a negative review on the first page? Or what choices will you make if Google shows a bland, irrelevant Brand SERP, even after you have put in the time, resources, and effort to revamp it?

When first building their Brand SERP, many people become frustrated or discouraged at how much effort is required and how long the process takes. The methods I've explained in this book are incredibly powerful, but like anything worth doing, they require time, effort, dedication, and patience. Even with massive input, your timeframe is months and years, rather than days.

It's only natural for some businesses to cheat to save time and resources and "beat the system." But if you are tempted, ask yourself this: *What is the potential cost?* The answer: *Your entire brand reputation.*

This is one of the most important points I impress upon clients: when working on your Brand SERP (and therefore your brand's credibility in the eyes of your audience and Google) do not, under any circumstances, try to cheat and sneak around Google. Notice I used the words "try to."

In this context, shortcuts rarely work for short-term benefits and never work for long-term ones. In other areas of life—say when taking a test or playing a game—cheating is a calculated risk, one with either a positive or negative outcome. However, your Brand SERP is different; cheating will always hit you where it hurts. The only uncertainty is how long it will take Google to find and reflect your deceit in your Brand SERP for your audience to see. This "trickery" against Google will cause long-term damage to your credibility with your audience and tarnish your trustworthiness with Google.

When you cheat your Brand SERP, you are cheating in full and open view of Google. Your Brand SERP is Google's representation of your reputation. Cheat on that and you'll end up shooting yourself in the foot. Imagine you're cheating on a test while your teacher stares at you the whole time. Like the teacher, Google will catch you no matter how smart you think your tactics are. Google is watching you. It created the "game," and it is in control of the examination room. Google holds all of the cards, so if you want to win the "Google game," play the game by Google's rules.

Google controls your digital business card, and if you cheat, it will present you as a cheater to your real life audience. And *that* has the potential to kill your business.

Cheating at Google's Game

In SEO, cheat tactics are called Black Hat. Black Hat tactics are designed to find weaknesses in Google's algorithms and exploit them to create artificially improved results.

Ever since the start of the internet, people have developed Black Hat tactics to trick Google's algorithms. They have been able to "turn the tables" on Google. This is impressive, especially considering Google's multi-billion-dollar technology and reputation. Even so, these cheats aren't a sustainable marketing strategy for a legitimate business.

Black Hat tactics are designed to find weaknesses in Google's algorithms and exploit them to create artificially improved results.

Even though these techniques can bring short-term wins if Google has not immediately noticed your tricks, it will eventually cotton on and the brand reputation you worked so hard to build *will crumble*. Your Brand SERP will turn "sour" and may become negative quickly. At this point, you will totally lose Google's trust, and it will present you negatively on your Brand SERP. Just like in life, winning back trust you have lost is one of the hardest tasks you'll ever undertake.

You might think you can just close your website and start afresh. Wrong. Google remembers you and your brand as entities, meaning Google knows who you are and won't forget it. With the implementation of entity-based search (the Hummingbird update), any bad reputation you earned from cheating *will* follow your brand for the rest of its online life (so, forever).

The end of every cheater's story is the same: if you try to trick Google, you will sabotage your trustworthiness and "kill" your reputation, causing permanent damage to your Brand SERP. With this perspective, building a Brand SERP the correct way doesn't seem so laborious.

Black Hat Marketed as a Quick Fix

When trying to make their Brand SERP "sexy" or drown negative search results, brand owners will typically encounter agencies offering Black Hat tactics. It is understandable to see these cheating techniques as a "quick fix" to drown high-ranking unfavorable articles, reviews, or comments. Generally speaking, the Black Hat strategy will be to flood Google with so much new, positive content that the negative result gets pushed down and replaced. This often takes the form of paid-for articles or blog posts, which are very costly and rarely rank on a Brand SERP.

Google *wants* to show the most helpful, relevant, and valuable results to your audience. With that outlook, brand new content on irrelevant sites won't make sense to Google. And even if Google did think these additional sites provided value to your audience, the sheer volume of this mediocre content will mean it has little or

no impact on your Brand SERP—you can create 10 great articles about your brand, but Google cannot show them all.

Hiring a company that promises to remove a negative result in a few weeks may seem like a clever "hack," but their techniques make no sense in your Brand SERP strategy, nor do they make good business sense. These companies generally operate against Google's guidelines, which, of course, are not laws nor absolute orders. However, since you are asking Google to present your brand in a positive light, you are effectively playing its "game," and Google defines the rules. Break those rules at your own risk.

While Black Hat strategies can sometimes successfully break the rules and outsmart the algorithms over a short time period, the long-term effects are always negative for a legitimate business hoping to present their audience with a great "Google Business Card." If you are too obvious or greedy, Google may even *totally* ban your site short-term.

Setting aside your Brand SERP, you also must consider your human audience. If a spam article does rank, then how will your audience perceive it? With the internet full of spammers and scammers, users are constantly on high alert for malware and suspicious content. If your Brand SERP appears fake or cheated, readers will certainly get a bad impression of your brand and navigate away from you.

The Principal Self-Sabotaging Black Hat Strategies to Avoid

To refrain from damaging your reputation in Google's eyes, you should avoid three main categories of Black Hat tactics. Importantly, these serve as the antithesis to the three SEO pillars in the earlier chapter about SEO[1]:

1. Creating False Understanding: Placing false information on third-party sites trusted by Google (such as Wikipedia) to trick Google into believing misinformation and portraying you more favorably to its users.

2. Buying Credibility: Paying an individual or company to link to your content or provide you with fake reviews to make your brand seem more recommendable.

3. Feigning Suitability: Creating texts that are designed to trick Google into thinking you provide a relevant and helpful solution to its users when, in fact, you don't.

Black Hat tactics like these are a common form of cheating used by business owners to try and manipulate Google's appreciation of their brand and their content. As Google evolves and changes, so will the methods used to exploit its algorithm. New ideas and "SERP hacks" are created and tested every day, and although they sometimes work short term, in a world where Google understands who you are, it is extremely dangerous to associate your brand with them.

---

1   As a refresher, these three pillars are: Understanding, Credibility, and Sustainability.

The Fundamentals of Brand SERPs for Business

The next page details some of the most common cheats from 2021, many of which promise sure-fire "wins" on Brand SERPs. Assuming you have a long-term, customer-centric brand strategy, you should avoid them despite their popularity.

Constructing Artificial Credibility Through Private Blog Networks and Buying Links

Private Blog Networks, or PBNs, are dedicated websites that serve no other purpose than to post links to increase the rankings of one or more websites. Google uses links to help determine a website's credibility, so PBNs can potentially allow you to amplify a website's credibility artificially. However, while PBNs seem tempting, experienced consultants can spot them within minutes. This trick worked for years, but Google has gotten smarter. Now, PBNs are glaringly apparent to Google too.

Buying links goes hand-in-hand with using PBNs and is just as dangerous. When looking to improve your brand's credibility in Google's eyes, you may stumble across sellers who claim they can provide amazing, authoritative links for low prices. As with all SEO and Brand SERP tactics (and most things in life), if it looks too good to be true, then it is a too-good-to-be-true scam.

While these sellers will post links to your site for suspiciously affordable prices, the links will be obviously unnatural and will add absolutely no value to your brand. They will appear in irrelevant, scattered places across the internet, such as random forum threads, comment sections, directory links, and dubious websites. The seller may even post them on a PBN, which just compounds the problem.

Cheap links are a waste of money and a detriment to your brand. Not only will they fail in their main objective, but they'll signal to Google that you're manipulating the system.

To Spam or Not to Spam

It's not much of a question; spam is the wrong approach for any business building a respectable brand with long-term ambition. Once you are labeled as a cheat, it becomes difficult to repair this impression. In the summer of 2021, Google implemented a new spam-centric update to prevent link manipulation and content spam. Increasingly, if Google's algorithms classify your brand or website as spam, it will automatically exclude you from the search results without warning or notice. The best way to prevent this drastic consequence is to instead use traditional marketing strategies such as brand building and client satisfaction. Avoid Black Hat tactics like PBNs, automatically generated content, and cheap links.

Every single action you take, including any cheating tactics, is directly and forever tied to your brand, a.k.a. your biggest asset. If you attempt to cheat Google, your brand will be associated with this mistake forever.

Negative SEO

Some brands really push Black Hat to a darker level and aim to damage their competitor's Brand SERPs with negative SEO. While some use the term "negative SEO" as a synonym for Black Hat methods, they are not synonymous. Whereas Black Hat aims to improve the performance for an owned brand, negative SEO aims to attack and damage another brand's SEO. Someone who uses a negative SEO campaign against a competitor is aiming to convince Google's algorithms that the target brand is not credible or is using Black Hat cheat techniques. This could involve creating untrustworthy backlinks and pointing them towards their competitor, fabricating harsh 1-star reviews, or building fake duplicate websites in an attempt to damage their competitor's ranking. Some even go so far as to hack, or hire someone else to hack, their competitor's website and vandalize their SEO performance.

Avoid this approach. If you take a negative SEO approach to target your direct competitors, it's very possible that your competitor will catch you, and they will retaliate through negative SEO tactics of their own or even take legal action against you.

If you think you can be "sneaky" in your deception, you're wrong. Negative and Black Hat SEO always leave behind a permanent, identifiable digital footprint. Anything you implement today will be visible to Google, your competition, your audience, and the courts in 10 or 20 years' time.

Except for the rare exception, the legal system is not going to offer much help, even for the targets of these attacks. Unfortunately, involving lawyers typically does not solve the problem in a timely, productive manner. In fact, the opposite is true. The judicial process costs a fortune, wastes valuable time, and almost never ends in a win. Even at the best of times, the legal process is slow, costly, and cumbersome. In the context of the internet, legal proceedings get significantly worse.

Legal action is not a "quick fix." The better approach is to counter the attack online by working to absolutely dominate your own Brand SERP and leave no space for intruders.

While the law slowly evolves via legislation, the internet is changing constantly, thus the law never really keeps up. This problem is compounded by the fact that judges don't necessarily understand the new laws or have familiarity with how the internet actually works, which can slow down the legal proceedings or impact your chance of success. Then there's the additional complication of finding a lawyer who understands the situation enough to leverage the relevant legislation to win the case. And the killer problem is, even if you win the case, it will take years and cost a fortune to enforce the judgement. More often than not, the offending article will have been replaced on the SERP before the court case has any effect.

Whether tied to negative or Black Hat SEO, every single action you take, including any cheating tactics and court cases, is directly and forever tied to your brand, a.k.a. your biggest asset. If you attempt to cheat Google, your brand will be associated with this mistake forever. Google has been watching you since the first day you appeared online, and it's not about to "forget" about your brand.

We are playing Google's game, so for sustainable, long-term results, we must play by Google's rules. Google is a sophisticated machine that's continually getting smarter, making it increasingly difficult to trick or cheat. Risk-free shortcuts in Brand SERP management frankly do not exist, and in my experience, everyone who cheats on their Brand SERP always learns this same lesson:

Even if you "turn a trick" today, cleaning up the residual mess long term is far more costly than any short-term gains.

CONCLUSION

An online business presence is no longer optional; it's a necessity. Before customers make purchases and spend their money, they will always pull out their phones and do a quick informational search to evaluate a brand's message and reputation.

- What message does Google portray to your audience when they search your brand?
    - ◊ Are they able to learn the basics about you?
    - ◊ Is the information accurate?
- What does your "Google Business Card" look like?
    - ◊ Is the message clear? Convincing?

These questions can be the make or break of a sale. But beyond that, the answers to these questions can shape your entire digital content strategy.

Brand SERP optimisation is the foundation of your online brand management. Improvements to your Brand SERP have a domino effect, expanding out to improve your SEO performances and your overarching online marketing strategy. Getting the initial domino in place is crucial for the rest of the strategy to succeed. By improving your Google Business Card for your audience, the rest will naturally fall into place and your wider SEO, content strategy, and online reputation will become a triple-threat against your competitors.

You need to educate Google before it can present your audience with an accurate, positive, and convincing representation of your Brand SERP. The process is simple, but it requires you to invest time and resources into a meaningful and effective digital strategy that serves your Brand SERP.

In the competitive world of business, you don't want to leave your brand's message to chance, so you need to build a positive digital ecosystem and manage your Brand SERP proactively.

This process involves:

- Optimising
  ◊ Your Homepage
  ◊ Rich Sitelinks
  ◊ Your Social Media Accounts
  ◊ Google Ads
- Improving
  ◊ Search Results (the ones you control *and* those you don't)
  ◊ Your Content Strategy
  ◊ Audience Participation
- Employing
  ◊ Simple SEO Tactics across the board
- Engaging your audience with relevant content
- Avoiding
  ◊ Cutting Corners with Cheats

Since your Brand SERP reflects the world's opinion of your brand, you absolutely *must* develop a diverse, active, and attractive digital ecosystem that truly engages your audience. Any content you produce must support your brand, be relatable for your audience, and add at least one small brick to building a consistent, accurate, positive, and convincing brand message.

The anatomy of a Brand SERP is based on the fundamental principle of Darwinism. If your Brand SERP is imperfect, then it has evolved to be imperfect. Unlike Darwinism, you can take control and change the course of natural selection by adapting your brand's digital strategy.

You may be tempted to cut corners and cheat to expedite your online presence. Don't. Competitor envy will only hurt your credibility and long-term success. It's like a horse looking left and right during a race. Distracted like this, the horse will trip itself up. That's why they wear blinders: to focus on what they are doing, where they are, and where they are going. Until you've sorted out your own horse, put your competitors out of your mind and concentrate on your own Brand SERP.

Whatever the weaknesses and strengths, you can change the course of evolution and focus on your brand-building goals. From bluelinks to Rich Elements (Video Boxes, Twitter Boxes, and even Knowledge Panels), you now have the power to manipulate the anatomy of your Brand SERP and design your Google Business Card, making it a "sexy" and powerful asset for your business.

This book is exclusively about Google to keep the approach (relatively) uncomplicated. Even by narrowing the topic down to one search engine, there was a lot of content to cover in one book! But if you think back to the introduction, I mentioned that 1 billion people use Bing every month. This statistic means your Bing Business Card is incredibly important too and shouldn't be pushed to one side as an afterthought. Au contraire: up to 10% of your audience uses Bing, and some people use multiple search engines in tandem. Even if Google dominates the industry, other search engines can still provide value to your brand and shouldn't be dismissed.

Luckily, Bing and Google function in much the same manner, so everything you do to improve your Brand SERP on Google will help improve your Brand SERP on Bing (and vice versa). It's a two birds, one stone kind of win that will improve your business's online performance.

When you get it "right," both Bing and Google will represent you in a positive light to their users. Each search engine will offer you incredible insights into what their users (and your audience) value, while also providing you with an independent evaluation of how the world perceives your brand.

This book and my courses are only the first steps to demystifying how Google, Bing, Yahoo and other search engines depict online brands. As search engines continue to improve their techniques for learning about and representing brands, Brand SERP strategies will evolve. To stay up to date on how to maintain your Brand SERP so it presents an accurate, clear, and compelling representation of your brand, the ultimate weapon is the SaaS platform, Kalicube Pro, which uses fresh data and up-to-the-minute techniques.

Business is a competition of Darwinistic natural selection—the best Brand SERP wins, so build yours up now.

Alt Tag: The alternative text for an embedded graphic. This text is used by screen-readers for sight-impaired people to describe the image. Google uses it to better understand what the image shows. It is a field that can be filled out in HTML code.

Black Hat Tactics: Any technique, tactic, or strategy that aims to unfairly manipulate or "trick" Google's algorithms to create artificially improved results. Identifying these techniques is a major focus for Google and it strives to exclude any web content that uses them. In the context of Brand SERPs (and so in the context of your brand and its reputation in Google's eyes), Black Hat techniques should be avoided.

Commercial Search (also called transactional): A search query where the user expresses an explicit commercial intent. For example, when someone types the search query "Buy shoes," they have an explicit purchase intent.

Crawlable: The idea that Google can access all of the important pages through a simple and logical path from the homepage.

Digital Ecosystem: The online presence of a business, such as the brand's site, social media presence, content, public feedback (including social media and customer reviews), and any third-party statements about the brand.

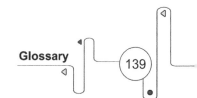

E-A-T: An acronym meaning Expertise, Authoritativeness, and Trustworthiness that Google uses as a measure of credibility.

Informational Search: Any search query where the user is looking to research and understand more about a brand or topic. In the context of Brand SERPs, a user may Google a brand name to learn about who they are, what they offer, and if they are trustworthy.

Knowledge Panel: An information box in the form of a panel that appears on the right-hand side when searching on your desktop computer. On mobile devices, they appear at the top. Knowledge Panels contain a summary of the important information that Google considers to be verified facts in response to a user's search query.

Leapfrogging: The process of improving positive results that appear below a negative result to push them up in the Brand SERP, thus pushing the bad result down.

Meta Title: The title of a webpage that the website owner provides in the HTML. Google uses this as the blue hyperlinked title in the SERP.

Meta Description: The description of a webpage that the website owner provides in the HTML. This is a summary of the information on the page. Google uses this to understand the page and will sometimes use it as the snippet description below the blue hyperlinked title in the SERP.

Navigational Search: Any search query where the user is looking for a specific website or brand. Most commonly performed with well-known brands like Facebook, this type of search occurs when a user already knows the brand and Googles it to access the brand's site.

The Fundamentals of Brand SERPs for Business

Negative SEO: The technique whereby a competitor actively implements tactics to help negative content appear on a Brand SERP or searches around a brand.

"People Also Ask" (PAA) Panel: A Google feature that provides a list of between two and five questions with their answers and a link to further information. Google wants to provide its users with information they didn't know they wanted/needed, so with PAA, users can read the panel instead of clicking the links to navigate to the answer.

Private Blog Networks (PBN): Multiple sites designed by a company or person to create authority for each of those sites purely based on the existence of other sites in the network. This is a Black Hat strategy.

Rich Element: A multimedia element known as a SERP Feature, such as Knowledge Panels, Twitter Boxes, Image Boxes, Video Boxes, etc.

Rich Sitelink: An expanded version of sitelinks, which includes the blue link text and a description (called a snippet).

Search Engine Optimisation (SEO): SEO is the art and science of persuading search engines such as Google, Bing, and Yahoo to recommend your content to their users as the best solution to their problem.

Semantic Triple: The term for identifying the "subject verb object" within content. Algorithms use semantic triples to understand what is being said, so writing accessible, clear, and correct sentences massively helps both Google and its users understand the meaning of your copy.

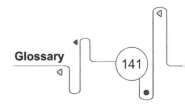

SERP: An acronym for Search Engine Results Page, the page Google displays after a user submits a search query into a search engine.

Siloing (also called categorisation): A technique used to stack or organise content vertically by topic. Effective and logical siloing allows search engines like Google to understand and digest information more effectively.

Sitelink: The technical term for the hyperlinks in the SERP that appear under the main blue hyperlink and lead to specific pages or subpages in a website. On a Brand SERP's homepage, they help users navigate to specific pages on a brand's website.

ACKNOWLEDGEMENTS

Life is never simple and is full of crossovers, so some people who could easily have been included in multiple sections just get one mention. :)

An enormous "thank you" to Anton Shulke for his help, support, and friendship over the last few years, and particularly his work on sticking with it and making both of the last two years "The Year of the Brand SERP"!

The Kalicube Team, past, present, and future, who have been an astonishing driving force behind making Brand SERPs a "thing" and making the Kalicube Pro platform so powerful. Katrina Bonete, Joan Buarao, Jesimar Estrada, Spencer Bohol, Ed Gestano, Cheene, Mary Ann Buarrao, April Joy Boral, Ez, Rui, Joshua, Kent...We are just getting started!

Peers and colleagues in the digital marketing community who welcomed me with kindness, took my ideas seriously, and encouraged my endeavors. Particularly: Andrea Volpini, Gennaro Cuofano, Olesia Korobka, Dave Davies, Koray Gübür, Bill Slawski, Dawn Anderson, Dixon Jones, Lily Ray, Joost de Valk, Purna Virji, Lily Ray, Rand Fishkin, Ted Rubin, Ryan Foland, David Avrin, Simon Cox, Jono Alderson, Dan Saunders, David Amerland, Laurence O'Toole, Barry Adams, David Amerland, Mordy Oberstein, Cindy

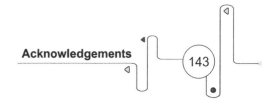

Krum, Craig Campbell, David Bain, Hannah Thorpe, Alexandra Tachalova, Mary Davies, Peter Mead, Nik Ranger, Paul Bongers, Erin Sparks, Marie Haynes, Aleyda Solis, Bibi Raven, and Loren Baker. Apologies to those I missed.

The people at Google and Bing who have generously supported me and shared insights directly in conversations and indirectly through all sorts of forums: John Mueller, Martin Splitt, Gary Illyes, Ali Alvi, Nathan Chalmers, Meenaz Merchant, and an especially big "thank you" to Frédéric Dubut and Fabrice Canel who both moved the needle for me back in 2019 with the opportunity to record "The Bing Series" of interviews in Redmond.

Every one of the 180+ guests on the podcast (and Kalicube Tuesdays) who taught me so much.

The editors who helped me write better: Melissa Fach, Danny Goodwin, Barry Schwartz, George Nguyen, and Erika Varagouli.

The amazing team at BrightRay Publishing (Emily Batdorf, Jamie Fleming, Scott Turman, and Zoe Rose) who got this book from a flaky start line to a finish line I am proud of and helped make Brand SERP optimisation accessible to everyone.

All of my friends who have been there through my personal, professional, and musical ups, downs, fun, foolishness, overambition, and provided genius insights that helped get, keep, or put me back on track. Particularly: Léonor-Jo Barnard, Véronique Barnard, Hugo Scott, Alan Sinclair, Dave Clayton, Nadia Sandi, Fred André, Josie Barnard, and Clio Barnard.

The Fundamentals of Brand SERPs for Business

For anyone I missed, I apologise in advance. Please let me know. I'll publish another book about Knowledge Panels soon. I can make amends there—it is a more academic topic, so is arguably a better place to be cited. In that context, this might actually be an unexpected "win" for you. :)

REFERENCES

"A Reminder on Qualifying Links and Our Link Spam Update."
Google Search Central Blog, July 26, 2021.
https://developers.google.com/search/blog/2021/07/link-
tagging-and-link-spam-update.

Clement, J. "Total Global Visitor Traffic to Bing.com 2021."
Statista, November 9, 2021.
https://www.statista.com/statistics/752270/range-of-bingcom-
based-on-unique-visitors/.

Desjardins, Jeff. "How Google Retains More Than 90% of Market
Share." *Business Insider*, April 23, 2018.
https://www.businessinsider.com/how-google-retains-more-
than-90-of-market-share-2018-4.

"The Internet and the Pandemic." Pew Research Center,
September 1, 2021.
https://www.pewresearch.org/internet/2021/09/01/the-internet-
and-the-pandemic/.

Johnson, Joseph. "Global Market Share of Search Engines 2010-
2021." Statista, October 8, 2021.
https://www.statista.com/statistics/216573/worldwide-market-
share-of-search-engines/.

"Kalicube Pro: Tools to Help You with Your Brand SERP." Kalicube
Pro. Accessed December 2021. https://kalicube.pro.

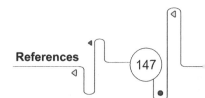

"Semrush Sensor—Google's Rank and Algorithm Tracking Tool."
Semrush. Accessed November 18, 2021.
https://www.semrush.com/sensor/.

"Social Media Fact Sheet." Pew Research Center, April 7, 2021.
https://www.pewresearch.org/internet/fact-sheet/social-
media/?menuItem=3814afe3-3f3c-4623-910b-8a6a37885ab8.

"Surprising Social Media Statistics—The 2021 Edition." Broadband
Search, 2021.
https://www.broadbandsearch.net/blog/social-media-facts-
statistics.

Ortiz-Ospina, Esteban. "The Rise of Social Media." Our World in
Data, September 18, 2019.
https://ourworldindata.org/rise-of-social-media#licence.

Jason Barnard, dubbed "The Brand SERP Guy" for his niche expertise, is a digital marketer who specialises in Brand SERP optimisation and Knowledge Panel management.

He is founder and CEO at Kalicube, a groundbreaking digital marketing agency and accompanying SaaS platform that helps clients optimise their Brand SERPs and manage their Knowledge Panels.

The podcast, "With Jason Barnard..." has become a weekly staple in the digital marketing community. Prominent guests include Rand Fishkin, Barry Schwartz, Ted Rubin, Winnie Sun, Eric Enge, Joost de Valk, Aleyda Solis, and Bill Slawski.

Jason is a regular contributor to leading digital marketing publications, such as *Search Engine Journal* and *Search Engine Land*, and he regularly writes for others including Wordlift, SE Ranking, SEMrush, Search Engine Watch, Searchmetrics, and Trustpilot. Jason is an internationally sought-after speaker and has recently appeared at BrightonSEO, PubCon, SMX series, and YoastCon.

Jason lives in Paris with his double bass.

72482019R20098